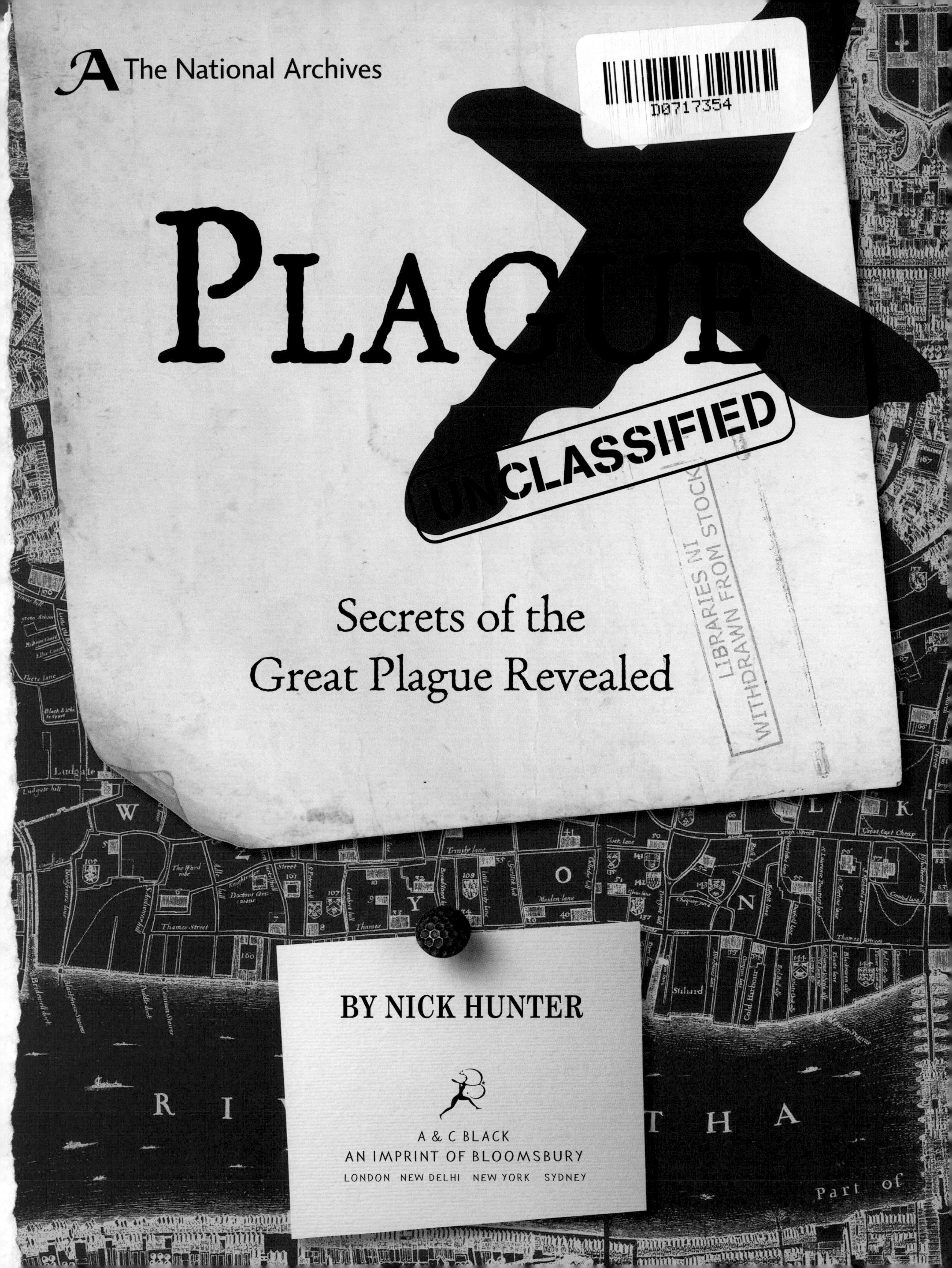

The National Archives
D0717354
PLAGUE
UNCLASSIFIED
LIBRARIES NI
WITHDRAWN FROM STOCK
Secrets of the
Great Plague Revealed
BY NICK HUNTER
A & C BLACK
AN IMPRINT OF BLOOMSBURY
LONDON NEW DELHI NEW YORK SYDNEY

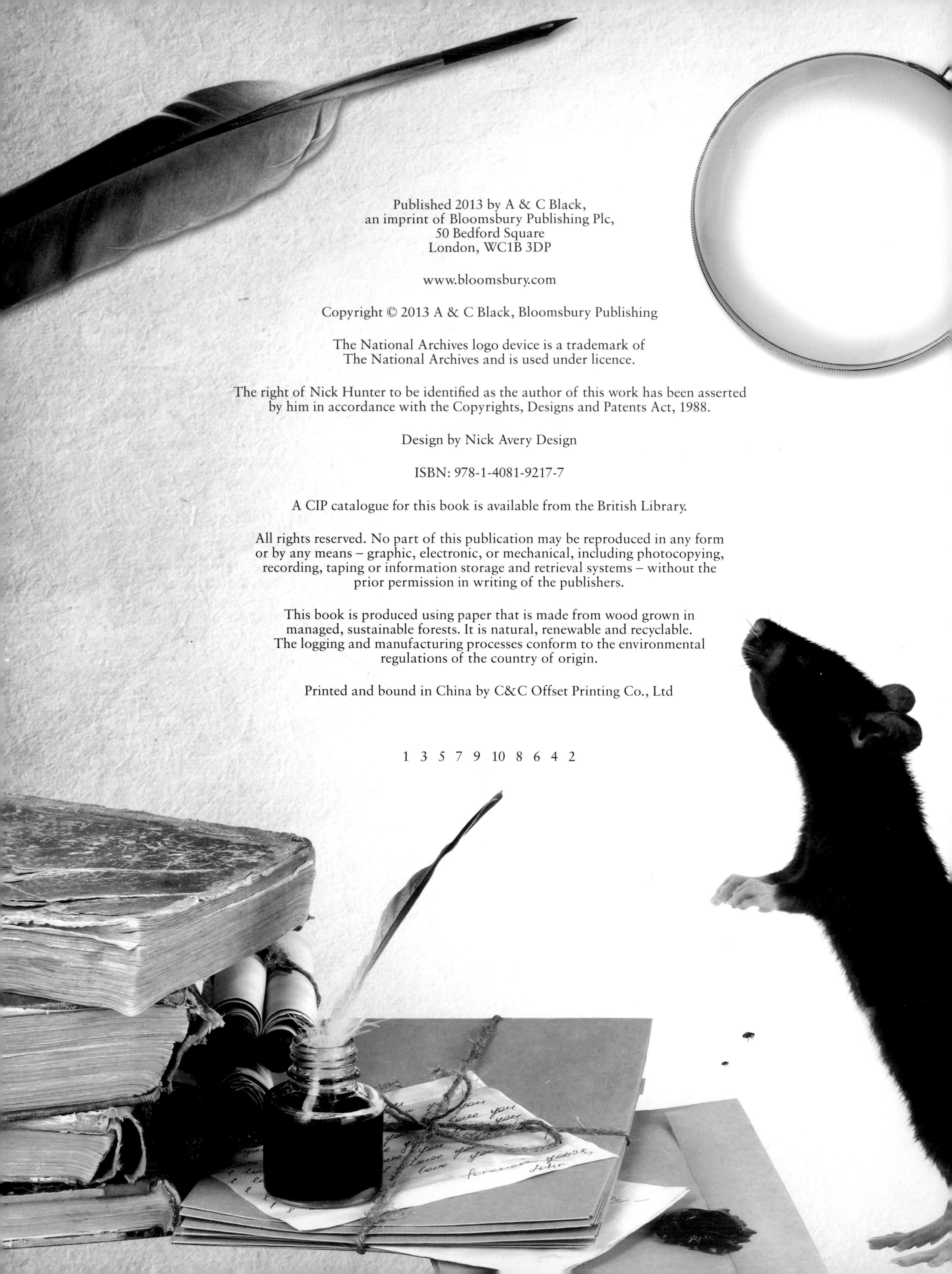

Published 2013 by A & C Black,
an imprint of Bloomsbury Publishing Plc,
50 Bedford Square
London, WC1B 3DP

www.bloomsbury.com

Design by Nick Avery Design

ISBN: 978-1-4081-9217-7

A CIP catalogue for this book is available from the British Library.

Printed and bound in China by C&C Offset Printing Co., Ltd

1 3 5 7 9 10 8 6 4 2

Contents

PLAGUE CITY

It was summer 1665, and a terrible plague gripped London. The city streets were filled with the smoke of bonfires to ward off the deadly disease. The clanging bells of the carts collecting the victims' bodies replaced the usual bustle of city life.

A terrible choice

As plague raged in London, a baby was secretly brought to Greenwich. The baby's parents had faced a terrible choice. Their other children had died of plague and they had sent the last child away. They might not see their baby again, but away from London the child had a chance of surviving.

Many Londoners faced decisions about life and death as the Great Plague swept through the city. In this book, we will discover the facts about the Great Plague and how it brought the city to its knees.

▶ Red crosses marked the houses infected with plague.

▲ Many people sent their children away from London to try and stop them catching the plague.

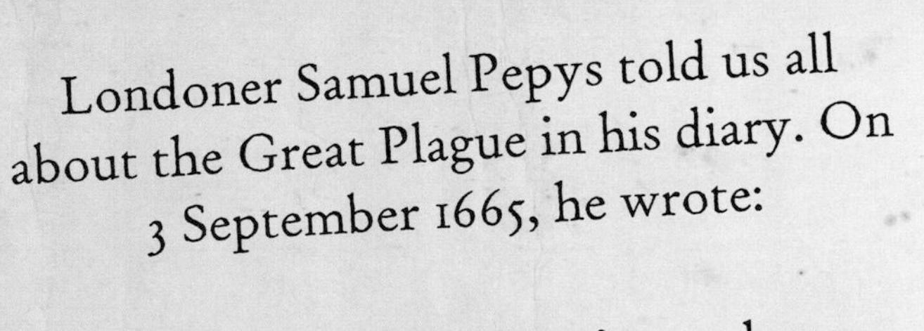

Londoner Samuel Pepys told us all about the Great Plague in his diary. On 3 September 1665, he wrote:

"a saddler ... did desire only to save the life of this little child; and so prevailed to have it received ... into the arms of a friend, who brought it ... to Greenwich; where upon hearing the story, we did agree it should be permitted to be received and kept in the town."

Samuel Pepys

Samuel Pepys

▲ *Plague victims being buried in 1665.*

Plague in History

The plague had paid regular visits to London for hundreds of years. In the 1340s, the Black Death arrived from Asia. This deadly outbreak of plague probably killed one out of three people in Europe. London was badly hit. Many villages were completely wiped from the map as everyone living there died of plague.

Plague facts

Some scholars believe that the Black Death was brought to Europe by troops from Asia. It is thought the troops hurled the bodies of plague victims over the wall of a city they were attacking.

Londoners were never safe from the plague. Every few years, the terrible disease would appear again in cities across Europe. In 1528, thousands of people died in just a few hours in the crowded streets of London.

God's punishment

Doctors were powerless to cure the plague. Some experts thought the plague was caused by bad smells and dirty air. Religious leaders said the plague was a punishment from God.

▼ People pray while carts carry away the dead during the plague in Milan, Italy in 1628.

◀ The people who faced the Black Death were very religious. They believed that the disease was sent by God to punish them.

▼ *A couple showing the boils and blisters of the dreaded Black Death.*

◀ *Plague doctors dressed like this were a familiar sight in plague-ravaged cities.*

Catching the plague

People in the past lived in fear of the sudden swellings around the armpits and groin that were sure signs that they had the plague. Other signs were a high temperature, vomiting, and pains all over the body. Once the plague appeared, there was nothing to do but hope they would survive it.

We now know much more about plague than the doctors of Medieval Europe or Londoners of the 1660s. It is caused not by bad air, but by a bite from an infected flea.

From rats to humans

The fleas were carried around Europe's crowded cities by the black rats that scuttled in the streets and under the floorboards. The fleas lived on the rats but would jump to humans if there were no living rats nearby. In a crowded city, just one flea could infect a number of people. The disease would quickly become an epidemic.

Plague facts

Early attempts to cure the plague included mixtures made using poison from snakes, scorpions, and frogs. People believed they would remove the poison of the plague. Not surprisingly, this did not work.

▶ *The humble black rat carried the plague into homes and crowded streets.*

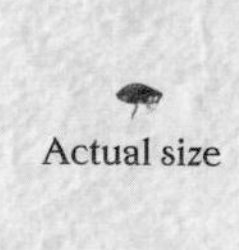

Actual size

A medieval doctor uses a scented sponge to protect him from the bad air of the plague.

London in the 1660s

If you had visited London in the 1660s, you would have been amazed by the huge and bustling city. London was one of the biggest cities in Europe and its streets were crowded with people; from the rich in their carriages to the poorest of the poor.

New buildings appeared wherever there was a patch of clear ground and were packed tightly together. Ships brought goods and people from all over the world to London's docks. They also carried rats and fleas that made their homes in the stinking streets of London.

Stinking city

The city was incredibly dirty and smelly. All the waste and rubbish was thrown out into the streets, where it would mix with mess left by horses and other animals. Only the rich would have any water supply in their homes. London's streets and houses were perfect places for rats and germs to breed and spread disease across the city.

▲ Poo from humans, horses and other animals was a constant hazard on London's streets.

▶ London as it appeared from across the filthy River Thames in the 1660s.

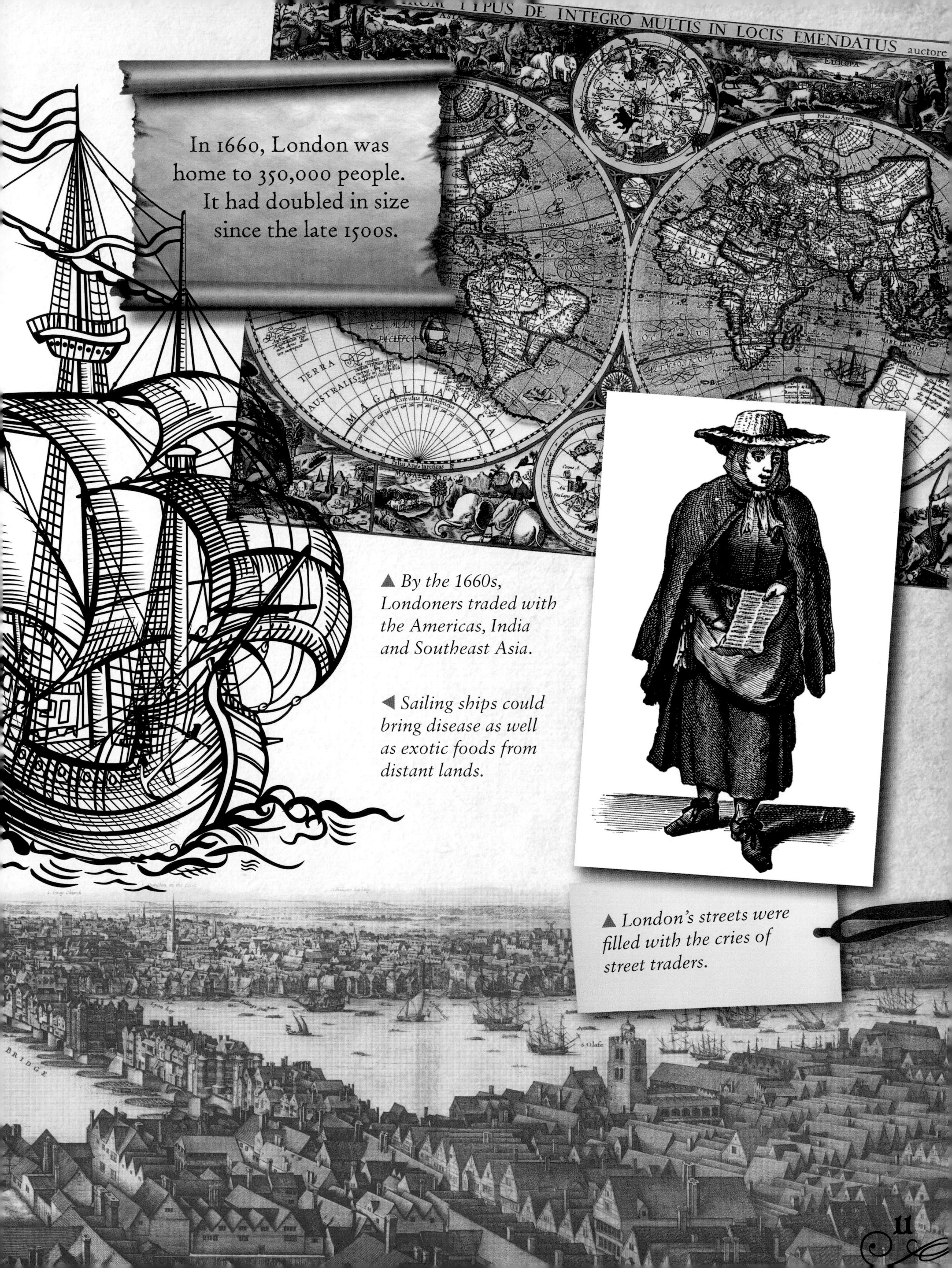

In 1660, London was home to 350,000 people. It had doubled in size since the late 1500s.

▲ *By the 1660s, Londoners traded with the Americas, India and Southeast Asia.*

◀ *Sailing ships could bring disease as well as exotic foods from distant lands.*

▲ *London's streets were filled with the cries of street traders.*

WARNINGS OF PLAGUE

In late 1664, a bright comet appeared in the night sky over London. For most people of the time, this was a very bad sign. Everyone believed that comets were an omen of bad things to come, and England was due some bad luck.

Preachers and people who thought they could see into the future had been predicting disaster for years. The crisis that followed the English Civil War had only just ended in 1660, when King Charles II came to the throne. Rebels had beheaded his father, Charles I, in 1649. Both sides believed that God would punish England for the sins of the civil war, and for the wicked ways of Londoners in particular.

▲ *In 1651, mystic William Lilly predicted plague and fire would destroy London. He was right about both.*

Getting closer

There were rumours of plague in cities across the sea, such as Amsterdam. Plague spread along trading routes. People waited nervously to see if it would suddenly appear in London.

◀ *King Charles II was known as the "Merry Monarch" because of his love of parties.*

▲ *Comets were often seen as a sign of bad luck in the past. We now know that they are simply lumps of ice and rock flying through space.*

The plague getting nearer was big news, as Daniel Defoe recorded in his novel, *A Journal of the Plague Year:*

"It was about the beginning of September, 1664, that I, among the rest of my neighbours, heard … that the plague was returned again in Holland; for it had been very violent there, and particularly at Amsterdam and Rotterdam, in the year 1663."

◀ *The new king Charles II came to power in 1660, ending 20 years of war that had split the country.*

Plague comes to London

The government understood that ships from overseas could bring the plague to London, although they didn't realize that it was the rats that the ships carried which brought the disease. Ships arriving in London were quarantined to try and stop the plague spreading.

Despite this safety measure, a few cases of plague were reported in 1664. However, the winter was cold and the disease did not seem to spread. People started to hope that London had escaped this time.

The cover up

As spring came, so did more reports of plague in the poorest areas such as St Giles. At first, everyone kept quiet about the plague. Reports of plague were bad for business. Trade with the rest of the world would stop and people would be too scared to leave their homes. But the more people pretended there was no problem with the plague, the faster it spread.

▶ *The River Thames was the main highway of London, with sailing ships and barges moored along its banks.*

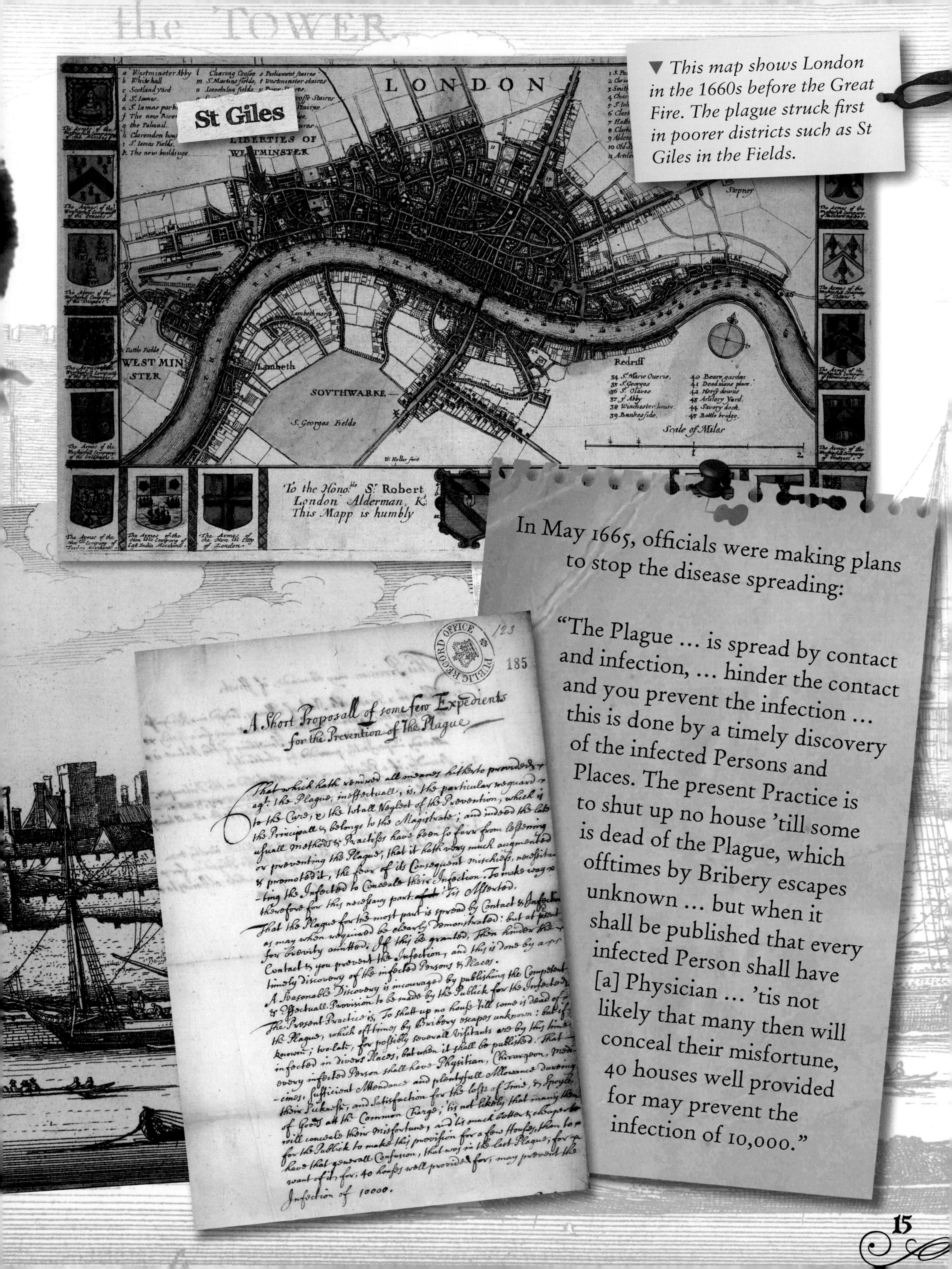

▼ *This map shows London in the 1660s before the Great Fire. The plague struck first in poorer districts such as St Giles in the Fields.*

In May 1665, officials were making plans to stop the disease spreading:

"The Plague ... is spread by contact and infection, ... hinder the contact and you prevent the infection ... this is done by a timely discovery of the infected Persons and Places. The present Practice is to shut up no house 'till some is dead of the Plague, which offtimes by Bribery escapes unknown ... but when it shall be published that every infected Person shall have [a] Physician ... 'tis not likely that many then will conceal their misfortune, 40 houses well provided for may prevent the infection of 10,000."

The spreading panic

In June, Londoners realized that all the warnings of plague were true. The disease started to spread from the poorer areas to the very heart of the city. People started to panic.

Theatres were ordered to close to prevent the disease spreading. People from plague-ridden areas were also stopped from travelling into other areas of the city. Rich people, who could afford to leave, fled from London. The poor were left behind to face the disease.

Samuel Pepys

A brush with plague

Not all the rich left the city. Samuel Pepys sent his family away but stayed himself. He had a close encounter with plague in June when the driver of his coach stopped in the street saying he was suddenly struck "very sick and almost blind" with the disease.

Plague facts

Deaths from plague were increasing all the time. Only 43 victims were recorded in the first week of June 1665, but by the beginning of July plague was killing almost 500 people per week.

LONDON'S Dreadful Visitation:
Or, A COLLECTION of All the
Bills of Mortality
For this Present Year:
Beginning the 27th of December 1664. and ending the 19th. of December following:
As also, The GENERAL or Whole years BILL:
According to the Report made to the KING's Most Excellent Majesty,
By the Company of Parish Clerks of London. &c.
LONDON:
Printed and are to be sold by E. Cotes living in Aldersgate-street, Printer to the said Company 1665.

▶ People believed smoking would protect them from the plague.

▼ Bills of Mortality listed how many people had died from plague each week.

◀ Bodies were lifted on to carts like these for burial.

▲ The rich fled to their country homes and to stay with friends away from London. In this picture, the plague is represented by skeletons.

Plague rules

No one knew exactly how the plague was spread. However, the authorities could see that plague was more likely to strike in dirty, crowded parts of the city. They brought in strict rules to stop the disease spreading:

RULES and ORDERS

To be obſerved by all Juſtices of Peace, Mayors, Bayliffs, and other Officers, for prevention of the ſpreading of the Infection of the PLAGUE.

Publiſhed by His Majeſties ſpecial Command.

1. You are to take care, That no ſtranger be permitted to lodge or abide in any City, Town, or Village without a ſufficient Certificate of health, and the conſent of the next Juſtice of Peace, or chief Magiſtrate (if within a Corporation) which ſaid Certificate to be made by the Miniſter and Church-wardens of the Pariſh from whence ſuch perſon came, and confirmed under the Hand and Seal of the next Juſtice of Peace to the ſaid Pariſh.

2. That no old Houſhold-Goods whatſoever be received into any City, Burrough, Town, Village or Hamlet, coming from any place ſuſpected to be Infected with the Plague, without ſufficient Certificate.

3. That all publique Meetings and Concourſes of people, as much as may be (eſpecially to Funerals, Wakes or Revels) be Prohibited, where there is any ſuſpicion of the Plague.

4. That no Vagabonds nor Beggers be permitted to go and wander about the Countrey, or in any other City or place; and, That you appoint Watching and Warding for that end; and that all publique places (eſpecially Streets and Paſſages) be kept ſweet and clean; and that all Layſtalls, Dunghills, and Slaughter-houſes near any Dwellings be removed to places more remote.

5. That Order be given to all Houſholders to keep their Dwelling-houſes ſweet and clean, and to keep ſhut all windows opening towards Infected houſes.

▲ *This list of rules for dealing with plague was produced in 1666. It tells us what action the government took to tackle the disease.*

- **Gatherings of people, even for funerals were banned.**
- **Streets were to be kept clean at all times.**
- **Food in shops and markets was not allowed to rot.**

Filthy streets and rotting food attracted the rats that spread the plague, even if Londoners did not know that at the time.

Searching the sick

People called "Searchers and Examiners" had to inspect the sick for signs of plague such as: "Swellings or Risings under the Ears or Arm-pits". Those who had plague would then be taken to pest houses, or hospitals, where they could not pass the disease to others. There were even rules about bodies of plague victims not being buried in churchyards but in special burial sites.

◀ *This horrible figure is carved on the remains of a charnel house in France, where the bodies of plague victims were kept.*

◀ *Pest houses were little more than sheds, away from the city, where sufferers were sent. Most of them never returned.*

hat Fires in moveable Pans, or otherwise, be made in all necessary publique Meeting
ient Fumes to correct the Air be burnt thereon.
That care be taken that no unwholsom Meats, stinking Fish, Flesh, musty Corn, or any
osed to sale in any Shops or Markets.
That no Swine, Dogs, Cats, or tame Pigeons be permitted to pass up and down in
, in places Infected.
That the Laws against Inn-Mates be forthwith put in strict execution, and that no m
are absolutely necessary in each City or place, especially during the continuance of this p
10. That each City and Town forthwith provide some convenient place remote from the
uts, or Sheds may be Erected, to be in readiness in case any Infection should break out;
, That able and faithful Searchers and Examiners be forthwith provided and Sworn to s
the usual signs of the Plague, viz. Swellings or Risings under the Ears or Arm-pi
lains, Carbuncles, or little Spots, either on the Breast or back, commonly called Token
11. That if any House be Infected, the sick person or persons be forthwith removed to the
uts, for the preservation of the rest of the Family: And that such house (though none be
ourty days, and have a Red Cross, and Lord have mercy upon us, in Capital Letters affixe
ppointed, as well to find them necessaries, as to keep them from conversing with the four
12. That at the opening of each Infected house (after the expiration of the said Fourty d
n the said door, there to remain Twenty days more; during which time, or at least befo
odge therein, That the said house be well Fumed, Washed and Whited all over withi
lothes, or Houshold stuff be removed out of the said house into any other house, for at lea
ess the persons so Infected have occasion to change their habitation.
13. That none dying of the Plague be buried in Churches, or Church-yards (unless th
place assigned for that use (where other bodies are not usually buried) Boarded or Paled
other convenient places, and that a good quantity of unslackt Lime be put into the Gra
such Graves be not after opened within the space of a year or more, lest they infect othe
14. That in case any City, Burrough, Town or Village be so Visited and Infected,
its own Poor, That then a Rate be forthwith made by the adjoyning Justices of t
very next Quarter Sessions, for that use, upon the neighbouring Parishes, according
ient Relief; want and nastiness being great occasio
tmost endeavours, not only to see these Directi
ften as you shall be required, but that you stri
her Officers, to execute their respective Du
rity against them according to Law.
, and such other persons as are necessa
your particular care and discretion.
only the Monethly Fasts, but that th
bed according to His Majesties Proc
the relief and necessities of the poor i
oth from amongst you and us.

LONDON,
d *Christopher Barker*, Printers to th
xcellent Majesty, 1666.

Here are examples of some of the rules and orders:

"Published by His Majesties Special Command

1. You are to take care that no stranger be permitted to lodge in any city ... without a sufficient certificate of health ...
2. That no household goods whatsoever to be received ... from any place suspected to be infected with the plague...
3. That all public meetings ... be prohibited...
4. That no vagabonds nor beggars be permitted to ... wander about the country...
5. That order be given to all householders to keep their dwelling[s]... sweet and clean..."

SIGN OF THE RED CROSS

The strictest rules affected houses where someone had already caught the disease. People were not allowed to enter or leave the house, even if they showed no sign of plague. The ground floor windows and door would be nailed shut, and the door was marked with a red cross and the words, "Lord have mercy upon this house".

◀ *Plague victims shut up in their houses needed regular supplies of food to keep them alive.*

People who were locked in their houses could not work or get food. Although they were promised help with food, fear of catching the plague kept helpers away from the infected households. Some victims died of starvation rather than plague.

Foul fumes

After 40 days, the houses were opened and foul-smelling mixtures were burned to cleanse them. This seemed to work probably because the disgusting smell was too much even for the rats.

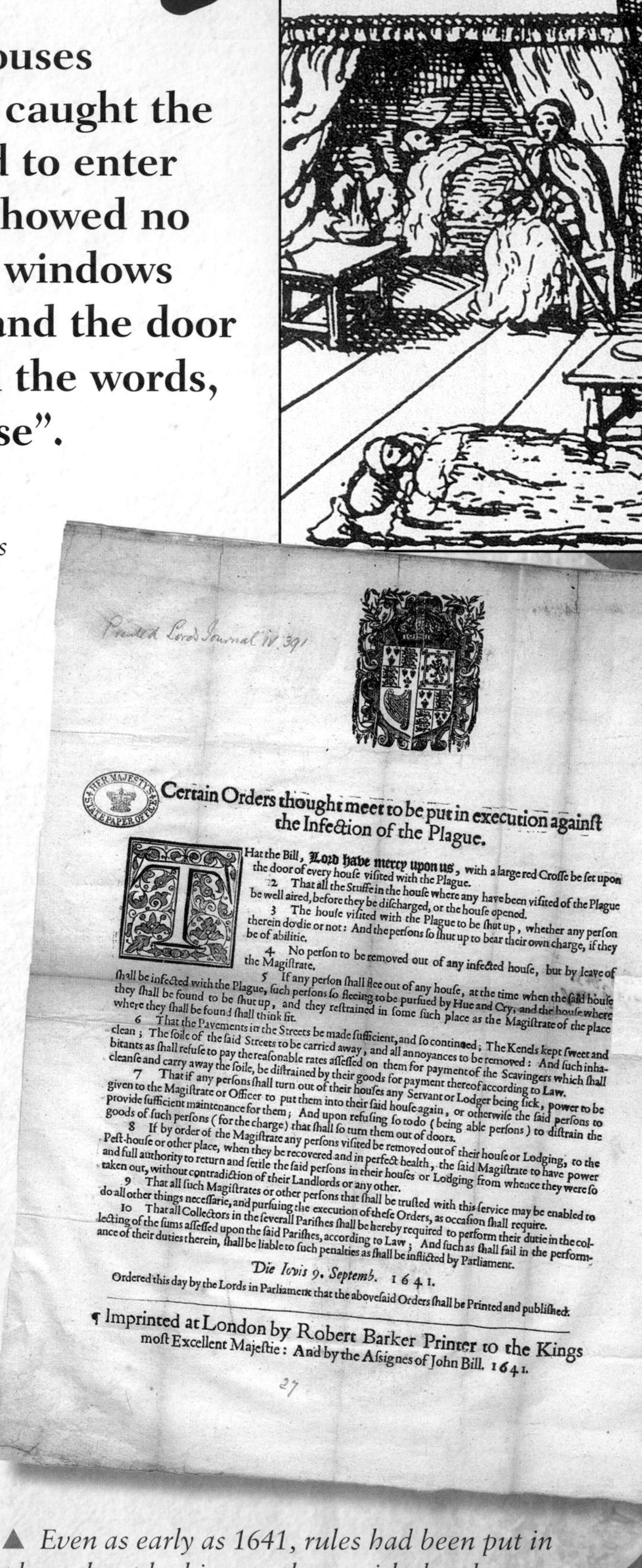

Certain Orders thought meet to be put in execution againſt the Infection of the Plague.

THat the Bill, **Lord have mercy upon us**, with a large red Croſſe be ſet upon the door of every houſe viſited with the Plague.

2 That all the Stuffe in the houſe where any have been viſited of the Plague be well aired, before they be diſcharged, or the houſe opened.

3 The houſe viſited with the Plague to be ſhut up, whether any perſon therein do die or not: And the perſons ſo ſhut up to bear their own charge, if they be of abilitie.

4 No perſon to be removed out of any infected houſe, but by leave of the Magiſtrate.

5 If any perſon ſhall flee out of any houſe, at the time when the ſaid houſe ſhall be infected with the Plague, ſuch perſons ſo fleeing to be purſued by Hue and Cry, and the houſe where they ſhall be found to be ſhut up, and they reſtrained in ſome ſuch place as the Magiſtrate of the place where they ſhall be found ſhall think fit.

6 That the Pavements in the Streets be made ſufficient, and ſo continued; The Kenels kept ſweet and clean; The ſoile of the ſaid Streets to be carried away, and all annoyances to be removed: And ſuch inhabitants as ſhall refuſe to pay the reaſonable rates aſſeſſed on them for payment of the Scavingers which ſhall cleanſe and carry away the ſoile, be diſtrained by their goods for payment thereof according to Law.

7 That if any perſons ſhall turn out of their houſes any Servant or Lodger being ſick, power to be given to the Magiſtrate or Officer to put them into their ſaid houſe again, or otherwiſe the ſaid perſons to provide ſufficient maintenance for them; And upon refuſing ſo to do (being able perſons) to diſtrain the goods of ſuch perſons (for the charge) that ſhall ſo turn them out of doors.

8 If by order of the Magiſtrate any perſons viſited be removed out of their houſe or Lodging, to the Peſt-houſe or other place, when they be recovered and in perfect health, the ſaid Magiſtrate to have power and full authority to return and ſettle the ſaid perſons in their houſes or Lodging from whence they were ſo taken out, without contradiction of their Landlords or any other.

9 That all ſuch Magiſtrates or other perſons that ſhall be truſted with this ſervice may be enabled to do all other things neceſſarie, and purſuing the execution of theſe Orders, as occaſion ſhall require.

10 That all Collectors in the ſeverall Pariſhes ſhall be hereby required to perform their dutie in the collecting of the ſums aſſeſſed upon the ſaid Pariſhes, according to Law; And ſuch as ſhall fail in the performance of their duties therein, ſhall be liable to ſuch penalties as ſhall be inflicted by Parliament.

Die Iovis 9. Septemb. 1641.

Ordered this day by the Lords in Parliament that the abovesaid Orders ſhall be Printed and publiſhed.

¶ Imprinted at London by Robert Barker Printer to the Kings moſt Excellent Majeſtie: And by the Aſsignes of John Bill. 1641.

▲ *Even as early as 1641, rules had been put in place about locking up those with the plague.*

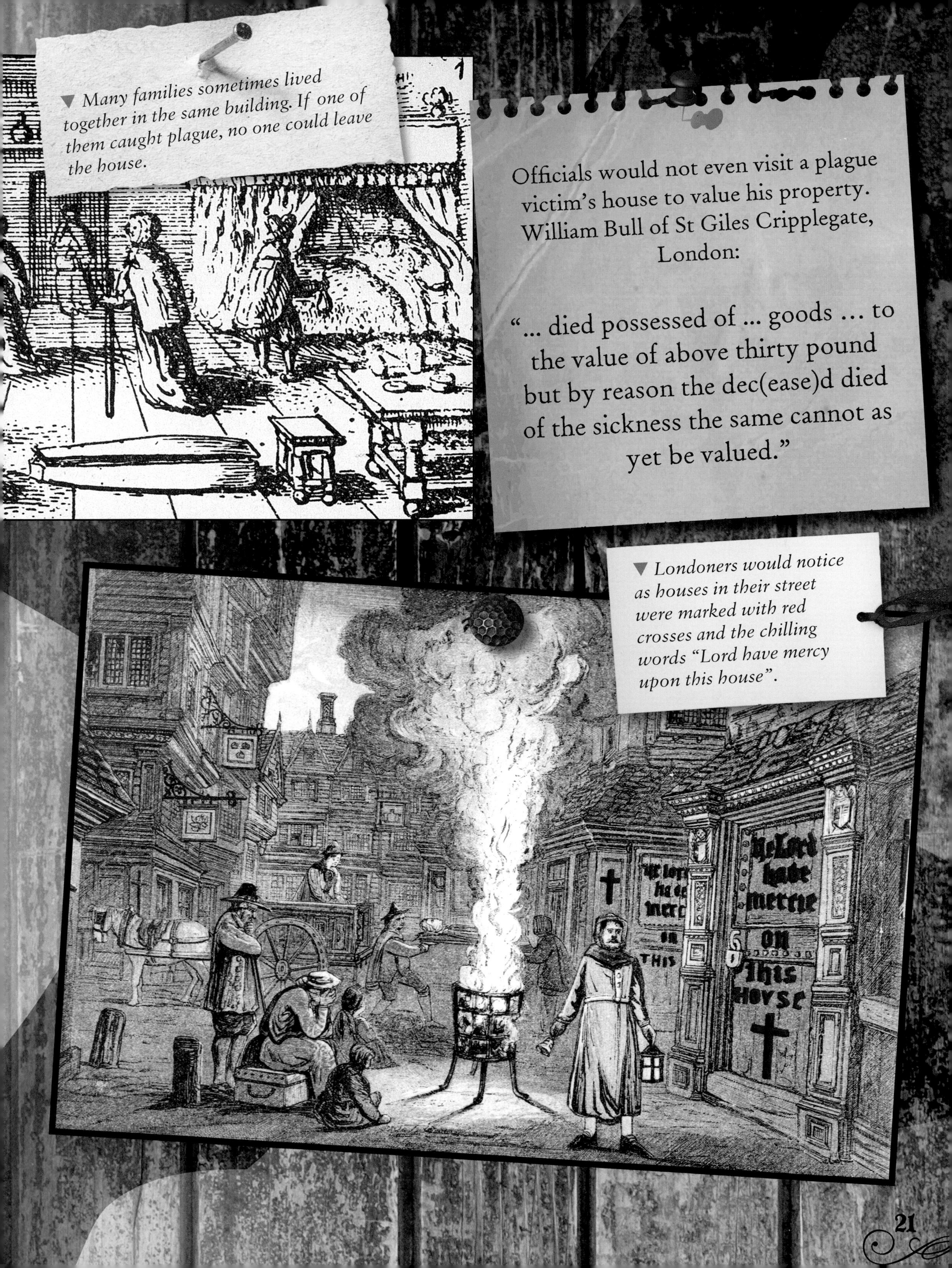

Many families sometimes lived together in the same building. If one of them caught plague, no one could leave the house.

Officials would not even visit a plague victim's house to value his property. William Bull of St Giles Cripplegate, London:

"... died possessed of ... goods ... to the value of above thirty pound but by reason the dec(ease)d died of the sickness the same cannot as yet be valued."

Londoners would notice as houses in their street were marked with red crosses and the chilling words "Lord have mercy upon this house".

Fighting the plague

In spite of all the attempts to control the plague, the weekly numbers of victims continued to rise over the summer. In the last week of August there were more than 6,000 deaths. Fear of the plague haunted everyone. How could they avoid catching it? Was there any escape if they did catch it?

There were plenty of clever or cunning people with ideas about how to cure the plague. More than 40 books and pamphlets were produced, each giving different remedies. People scared of catching the plague were advised to take substances such as treacle every day to ward off the disease.

▲ *A spoonful of treacle was recommended by churches and some doctors as a way to ward off the plague.*

▼ *Anyone could put together a mixture of ingredients and call it a medicine. Many remedies appeared on the streets, but none of them could genuinely stop the plague.*

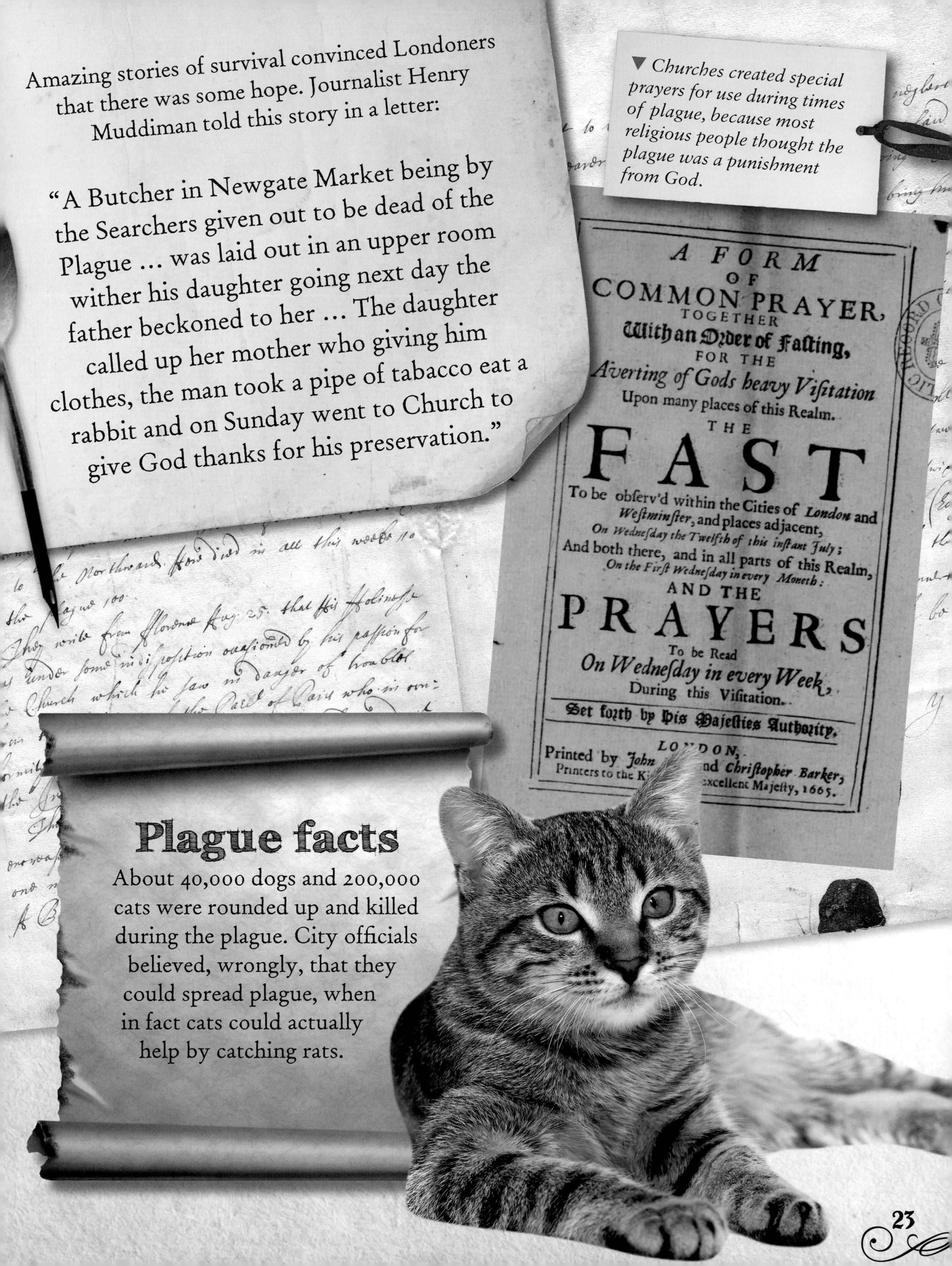

Amazing stories of survival convinced Londoners that there was some hope. Journalist Henry Muddiman told this story in a letter:

"A Butcher in Newgate Market being by the Searchers given out to be dead of the Plague ... was laid out in an upper room wither his daughter going next day the father beckoned to her ... The daughter called up her mother who giving him clothes, the man took a pipe of tabacco eat a rabbit and on Sunday went to Church to give God thanks for his preservation."

▼ *Churches created special prayers for use during times of plague, because most religious people thought the plague was a punishment from God.*

A FORM OF COMMON PRAYER, TOGETHER With an Order of Fasting, FOR THE Averting of Gods heavy Visitation Upon many places of this Realm.

THE FAST To be observ'd within the Cities of London and Westminster, and places adjacent, On Wednesday the Twelfth of this instant July; And both there, and in all parts of this Realm, On the First Wednesday in every Moneth:

AND THE PRAYERS To be Read On Wednesday in every Week, During this Visitation.

Set forth by His Majesties Authority.

LONDON, Printed by John ... and Christopher Barker, Printers to the K... ...xcellent Majesty, 1665.

Plague facts

About 40,000 dogs and 200,000 cats were rounded up and killed during the plague. City officials believed, wrongly, that they could spread plague, when in fact cats could actually help by catching rats.

THE SILENT CITY

Anyone walking the deserted streets of London when the plague was at its worst would have been shocked by the silent, ghostly city. Fires burning in the streets were supposed to clean the air. They filled the city with a smoky fog.

Most people stayed at home. They only went outside if they really had to, and all the shops and markets were closed anyway. Everyone walked down the middle of the street, where the dirt and rubbish usually collected. They wanted to be as far as possible from the houses that might contain plague.

Collecting the dead

The streets were empty of the horses, carts and carriages that would have normally filled them. Only the wheels of the carts collecting the dead bodies for burial could be heard clattering along the cobbles.

◀ Drivers of the plague carts used these bells to warn people that they were coming.

▲ "Bring out your dead!" calls the cart driver, while the grave digger waits to bury the bodies.

◀ Bodies of plague victims were carried to pits on the edge of the city.

Samuel Pepys wrote about the deserted city in his diary on 28 August 1665:

"But now, how few people I see, and those walking like people that have taken leave of the world … I to the Exchange, and I think there was not 50 people upon it …"

Samuel Pepys

John Allin's letters

Londoners who stayed in the city as the plague took hold grew more and more scared. Every week the disease struck closer to their homes.

▲ Lots of bodies were buried in mass graves called plague pits.

Clergyman John Allin wrote about his fears in letters to friends.

"I am troubled at the approach of the sickness nearer every week, and at a new burying place which they have made near us ... " (11 August 1665)

Allin recorded the rising numbers of victims, taken from the official Bills of Mortality.

"I am, through mercy, yet well in midst of death, and that, too, approaching nearer and nearer: not many doors off, and the [burial] pit open daily within view of my chamber window." (24 August 1665)

Too close to home

As the summer went on, everyone knew family or friends who had caught the plague. Allin wrote that his brother had felt ill on Sunday evening, feeling a "stiffness under his ear" (a swollen gland). He was dead by Thursday.

The friends who received Allin's letters were nearly as scared as he was. As people didn't understand how the plague was spread, they were worried that the letters themselves might carry the plague. Allin told them not to worry:

"Were my pen infectious my hand would soon let it drop." (20 September 1665)

◀ A picture from the time shows the Angel of Death spreading its wings over London.

▼ On 7 September 1665, Allin wrote that the plague was "at the next door" on both sides of his house. The plague spread quickly in London's cramped streets.

◀ Allin wrote about the plague getting closer and closer along the cramped streets of London.

Breaking the rules

Throughout August and early September, there was no rain to clear the stinking air from London's streets. The poor, who had not been able to leave when the plague started to spread, were much more likely to die of the disease as they lived in the most cramped and rat-infested parts of the city.

▲ *A terrifying image of a plague hospital in Vienna, Austria in 1679.*

"Watchers" were ordered to make sure that people who had been shut into their houses did not get out. But some desperate people did escape out of windows and over rooftops. Fear of being shut up with relatives dying of plague drove some escapees to attack, or even murder the watchers who had imprisoned them.

◀ *There was no police force in London. Keeping order was a dangerous job as Londoners became more desperate.*

Paying the price

The city faced a big problem. How could the government afford to feed all the people trapped inside their homes? By August 1665, they couldn't even afford to board up all the houses affected by plague, as there were so many. By September, Samuel Pepys did not talk to anyone in the street, just in case they might be infected.

Thomas Povey, a government official, wrote that people's attitude to official rules and restrictions changed as the plague continued into the autumn:

"... there having dyed more than 300 in Brentford and Isleworth, and Death is now become so familiar, and the People so insensible of danger, that they look upon such as provide for the public safety, as Tyrants and Oppressors ..."

◀ Thomas Povey's original letter written on 8 October 1665.

▲ *Plague victims were a common sight on the streets as the city's officials struggled to keep order.*

◀ *Often the food that was promised to plague victims did not arrive, as healthy people were too scared of the plague to deliver it.*

BURYING THE DEAD

London's streets rang with the "doleful and ... continual" ringing of the bells that accompanied the plague carts, as John Allin described it. In some places, coffins were left piled in the streets, waiting to be buried.

▶ *Churchyards filled to overflowing as the death toll mounted.*

▲ *Most plague burials took place at night in huge pits.*

Burials were supposed to happen at night. By late August 1665, there were so many deaths that this was impossible. Churchyards did not have room for all the dead bodies, and special pits had to be dug for burying plague victims. One pit in Houndsditch, East London, was 12 metres long, five metres wide and six metres deep. More than 1,000 bodies were buried there.

Funeral rights

Funeral processions in the city were banned, however many people ignored this law. This was partly out of respect for the victims, but also to rebel against the officials in charge. The wealthy lawmakers made strict rules for ordinary people, while they themselves could leave the city whenever they liked.

Writer John Evelyn was shocked when he visited London in September 1665:

"I went all along the City & suburbs from Kent Street to St. James's, a dismal passage & dangerous, to see so many coffins exposed in the streets ... & all in mournful silence, as not knowing whose turn might be next."

John Evelyn

▼ *An engraving from the 1660s shows people having an illegal funeral.*

THE RICH AND THE PLAGUE

King Charles II left London at the end of June, just as the plague was starting to spread. Many other important people also left the city around the same time. The wealthy people who stayed were careful not to come into contact with the disease. The Lord Mayor of London, for example, gave his orders from behind a glass case.

Samuel Pepys

Many wealthy Londoners were too scared to leave their houses, but Pepys carried on as normal with his life as an official in charge of the navy. He avoided public places as much as possible, including his church. Although he was saddened by all the talk of "death and nothing else", for Pepys and other well-off people, the plague was more of an inconvenience than a deadly enemy.

The King's chief minister, the Earl of Clarendon summed up his and his friends' experience of the plague:

"The greatest number of those who died consisted of women and children, and the lowest and poorest sort of the people . . . Not many of wealth or quality or much conversation [were killed]."

◀ *The Earl of Clarendon didn't seem to think that poor people were important.*

At the end of 1665, Pepys wrote:

"I have never lived so merrily . . . as I have done this plague-time."

Samuel Pepys

▲ *Samuel Pepys' diary includes more than one million words, some of which are in code. It gives us a very clear picture of life during the plague.*

▲ *The ban on ships entering the port of London meant wine and other luxuries from Europe were in very short supply.*

◀ *The Royal Exchange was where merchants and business people met. In August, Pepys said that the usually bustling courtyard was almost empty.*

Plague doctors

Anyone walking through London during the plague might have come across the sinister beaked masks of the plague doctors, appearing out of the smoky darkness. Many of these doctors were known as "quacks" (frauds) because they didn't really have any medical training.

▶ *The terrifying uniform of the plague doctor was used across Europe during the 1600s.*

Instead they treated plague victims with various herbs and potions. These included strange and even made-up ingredients such as powdered unicorn horn.

Even the trained doctors could not help the victims very much. Their cures for plague included using leeches to suck out victims' infected blood or bursting the hideous boils of plague victims with sharp metal lances.

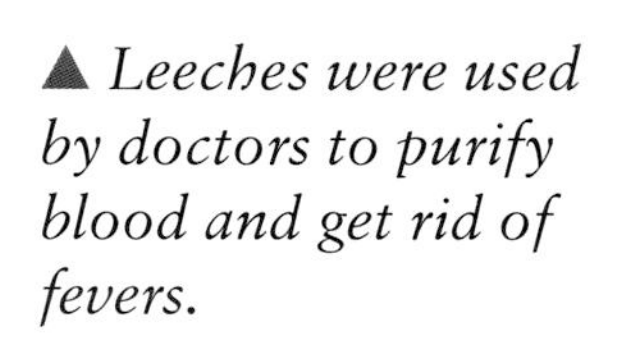

▲ *Leeches were used by doctors to purify blood and get rid of fevers.*

The doctor's uniform

The doctors' masks and long waxed robes were to protect them from the foul air in the homes of their patients. The doctors' robes actually worked because they stopped them being bitten by fleas, although no one knew that fleas actually caused the plague.

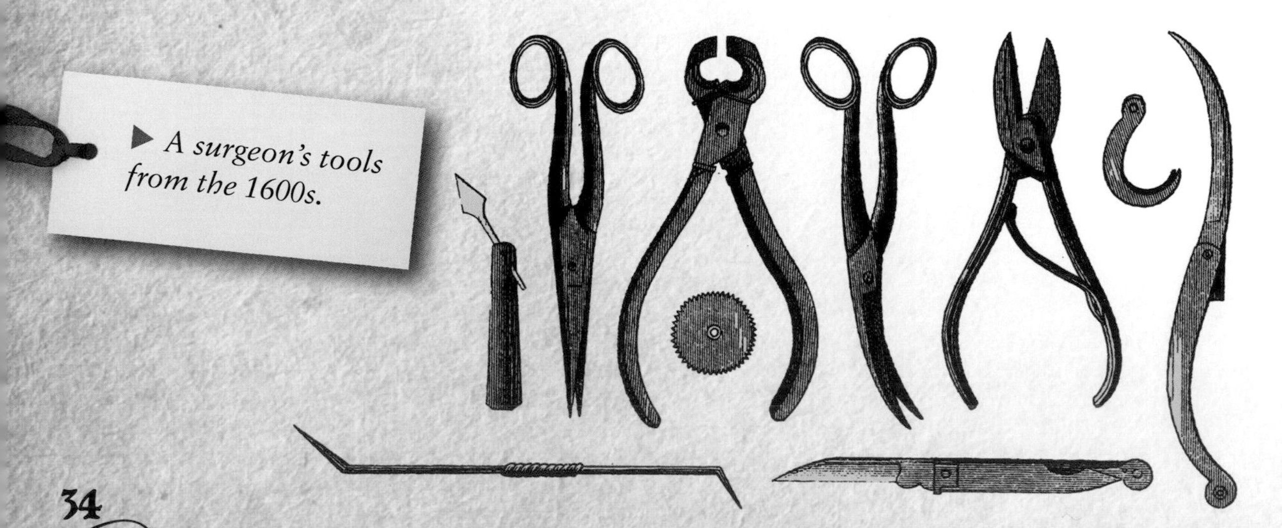

▶ *A surgeon's tools from the 1600s.*

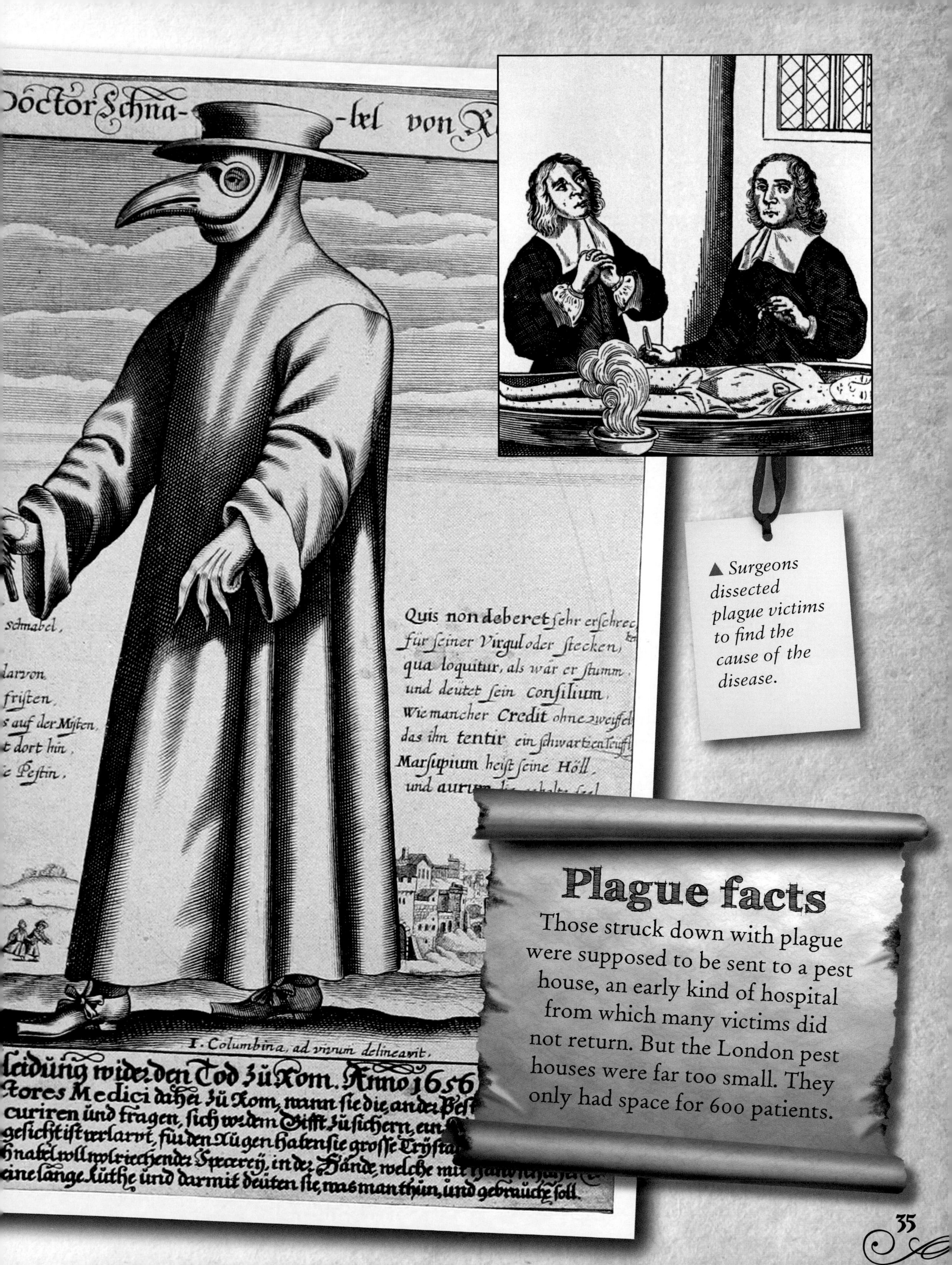

▲ *Surgeons dissected plague victims to find the cause of the disease.*

Plague facts

Those struck down with plague were supposed to be sent to a pest house, an early kind of hospital from which many victims did not return. But the London pest houses were far too small. They only had space for 600 patients.

Nathaniel Hodges: Treating the Plague

Unlike many other trained doctors, Nathaniel Hodges did not flee the plague. He stayed in London to treat his patients from his house in Walbrook by the River Thames. Twice, he believed he had caught the disease, but both times Hodges escaped unharmed.

▲ *Hodges' special medicine included lozenges made of myrrh, cinnamon and angelica root.*

Hodges had strong ideas about how to stop the spread of plague. He disagreed with the idea of shutting up sick and well people together, as he believed (wrongly) that the plague was passed from person to person through the air. Before visiting each patient he took a special medicine to protect himself. He also burned a mixture of resinous woods and herbs in each house he visited, which he believed would clear the plague from the air.

Hodges' medicine

Hodges' treatments included draining blood from his patients and bursting their blisters to release the plague. He also told plague victims to drink plenty of wine, as he believed this would help them to sweat out the sickness. Hodges was a highly trained doctor, but many of his ideas were no more useful than the potions and charms of the "quacks" that he hated so much.

▼ *Hodges took his own advice and drank plenty of Spanish wine to protect himself from plague.*

▼ *Hodges explained his beliefs about plague in this book.*

[1]

LOIMOLOGIA:

OR, AN

ACCOUNT, &c.

SECTION I.

the Riſe and *Progreſs of the late* PLAGUE.

THE Plague which we are now to give an Account of, diſcovered the Beginnings of its future Cruelties, about the Cloſe of the Year 1664; for Seaſon two or three Perſons died in one Family at *Weſtminſter*, attended

B

tended

Hodges was a great enemy of the "wicked impostors" who gave their patients medicines "more fatal than the plague". He also criticized the "barbarous wretches" who stole from victims while pretending to look after them.

▼ *The beak of the doctor's mask was filled with sweet-smelling substances such as lavender.*

TELLING THE STORY

The Great Plague of London was a terrible time for all those who lived and died during it, but it was just one of many plagues that swept across Britain and Europe at that time. We know a lot about the Great Plague because of the many books, reports and diaries that were written at the time.

Official papers and reports tell us about the facts of the plague and how the government tried to tackle the disease. They also give us a sense of the panic felt by even the most powerful people when faced with such an unstoppable disease.

Diaries and letters

We can find out what it was really like to live through the plague from the diaries of people like Samuel Pepys and John Evelyn. Letters were the only way of keeping in touch with friends and family, and they also carried news of the epidemic.

Gaps in the story

There are many gaps in what we know about the Great Plague. There were no photographs or videos in 1665. Many ordinary people could not read and write, so our view of those terrible months comes from the wealthier people of the time, who left written records.

▲ *Daniel Defoe was only a child in 1665, but he wrote a vivid story of that terrible year.*

Daniel Defoe's *A Journal of the Plague Year* tells the full story of 1665. But Defoe was only six years old at the time of the plague. His book was written much later and was supposed to be fiction, even if it was based on real life.

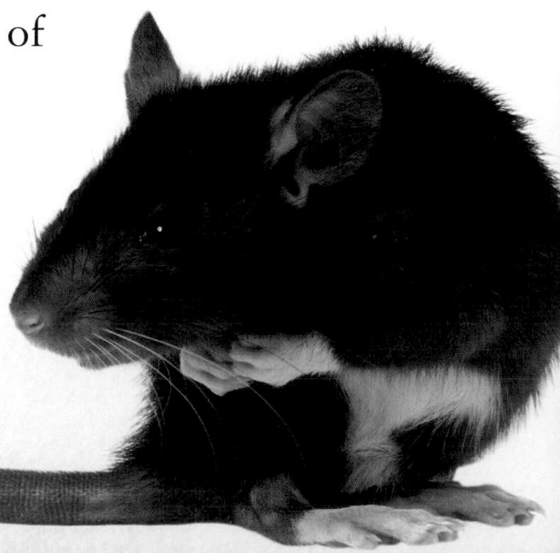

▼ *A scene from Defoe's* Journal of the Plague Year *shows one of many preachers who roamed the streets with terrifying warnings to Londoners.*

▲ *John Evelyn lived outside London but he wrote about visits to the stricken city in his diary.*

Desperate times . . . desperate measures

As the plague began to spread across the country, London's streets were still filled with panic and anxiety. By mid-September, the weekly number of deaths in and around London had reached 7,165. The people were terrified, and desperate to try any kind of cure or method of protection.

▲ Horseshoes have always been said to bring good luck.

Charms and magic

As it seemed doctors could not help, people resorted to magic and spells to save them. Londoners carried charms and amulets that would ward off the plague. Many of these charms included the word "Abracadabra", which was said to protect against evil and dark spells. The word has been linked with magic ever since.

Daniel Defoe's *A Journal of the Plague Year* sums up London's madness:

"[The Plague] came at last to such violence that the people sat still looking at one another, and seemed quite abandoned to despair . . . In a word, people began to give up themselves to their fears and to think that all regulations and methods were in vain ..."

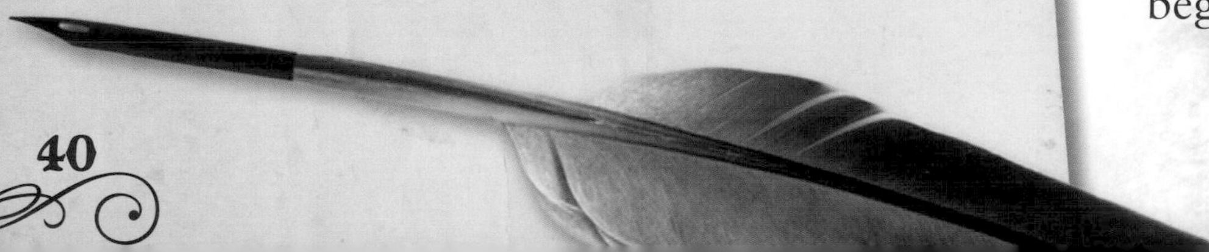

A new hope

People began to worry that the plague would be the end of London itself. But just as it seemed as if the horror would go on forever, things began to improve. On the 9 September 1665, Londoners welcomed the first rain for many weeks. By the end of September, the weekly death toll finally began to fall.

▶ People believed magic amulets could ward off plague.

▲ Many Londoners carried protective spells like this one from Germany.

The plague spreads

As the plague tightened its grip on London, the government tried desperately to stop the plague spreading from the city. Each town took different steps to try and keep the plague out. Leicester, for example, banned anyone entering from London unless they had a special certificate saying they were in good health.

Shutting doors and closing borders

Many people across Britain were so scared of catching the plague that they refused to take in members of their own families who had left London.

Scotland took no chances. The land border with England was closed completely. Ships arriving from infected areas were quarantined for 40 days before being allowed to dock.

Spreading by land and water

However, trade with London could not be stopped completely, and neither could the spread of the plague. The disease soon spread up and down the length of the River Thames. In late 1665 and early 1666 many towns were affected. In Colchester, about 50 miles (80 kilometres) from London, almost half its population died of plague. In some towns, plague sufferers were even accused of deliberately trying to spread the disease.

▶ *Family members outside London waited anxiously for news of their relatives.*

News of the plague spread by post. On 11 November 1665, one letter read:

"At Milbrook there has been an abundance of ravens croaking about the town. The oldest people say it has been so before when there was a great plague, so that they are much troubled, fearing the like again."

▲ *The plague was especially violent in the south and east of England. Wales and large parts of northern England were hardly affected.*

▲ *Country villages had little contact with the outside world and were often unharmed by the plague.*

▲ *People knew that outsiders could bring the plague with them.*

Plague village

Many villages had very little contact with large towns or people from London. They often escaped the plague. But the village of Eyam, Derbyshire, was not so lucky. The plague was brought to Eyam by fleas in a bundle of cloth from London. The village's tailor was the first victim in September 1665.

▲ *William Mompesson was the man behind Eyam's decision to face the plague alone.*

A difficult choice

After several deaths, the plague died down in the winter. It returned with force in June 1666. The village's rector William Mompesson persuaded the villagers that they should all go into quarantine, with no one arriving or leaving until the plague had passed.

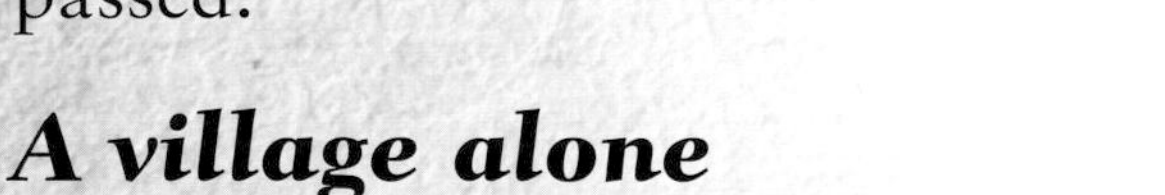

A village alone

If this was going to work, Eyam needed help. Mompesson arranged with the Earl of Devonshire that food would be left near the village. Villagers would then collect it. They left money for the food in a trough of water, as they believed this would prevent the plague from being accidentally passed on. The actions of Eyam's heroic people probably saved many lives in nearby communities.

◀ *Food had to be delivered so the villagers wouldn't starve to death.*

Plague facts

The people of Eyam paid a heavy price for their determination to save others from the plague. The village itself lost 260 of its 900 inhabitants from 89 different families, including Mompesson's wife Catherine.

◀ *Eyam's church was closed during the plague and services were held outside to prevent the spread of the disease.*

◀ *William Mompesson's wife was one of Eyam's many plague victims.*

▶ *The Boundary Stone in Eyam marked the edge of the area that was quarantined during the plague. Food and other goods would be left here for the village. The money to pay for these vital goods would be cleaned with water and vinegar and left in holes in the stone.*

Counting the Cost

Londoners could count the cost of the plague as it raged in the summer and autumn of 1665. Every week the official Bills of Mortality would tell them how many people had died. John Allin included the weekly death toll in his letters to friends. It must have been terrifying as the numbers kept rising.

Secret deaths

Even at the time people knew that the official figures were too low. There were good reasons for families not to report cases of plague. If someone raised the alarm, they would be shut into their homes with their sick relatives, making it even more likely they would catch the plague themselves.

The worst of all time?

The Great Plague of London was not the worst plague outbreak of all time, although it is probably the most famous one because there was so much written about it. Other outbreaks of plague in Europe, Asia and China killed tens of millions of people over the years.

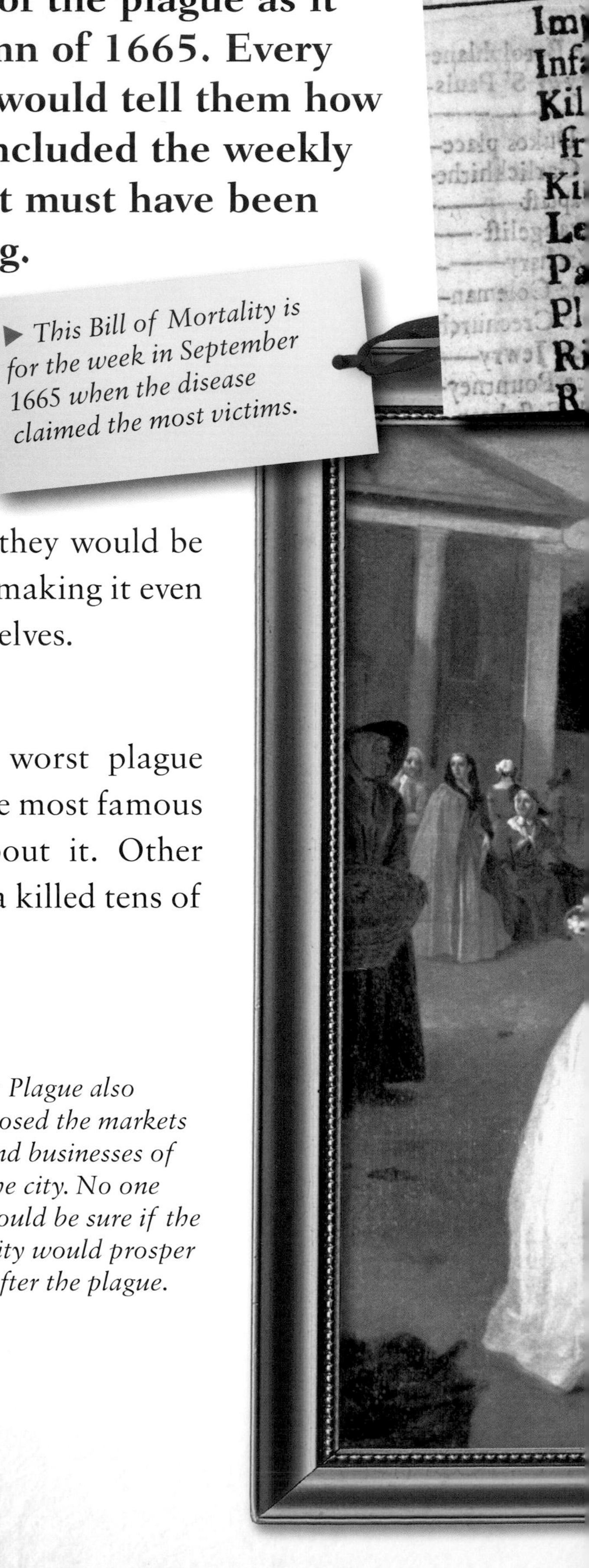

▶ This Bill of Mortality is for the week in September 1665 when the disease claimed the most victims.

▶ Plague also closed the markets and businesses of the city. No one could be sure if the city would prosper after the plague.

Plague facts

The total number of deaths during the Great Plague in London was 68,596 according to the official figures. The actual number was probably closer to 100,000, around one in seven of all Londoners.

this Week.
ume— 11
16
y a fall from the Bel-
Alhallows the Great— 1
il— 2
gy— 1
— 1
— 7165
— 17
—
of the Lights— 11

▲ *Many of those who died did not even have coffins to be buried in.*

FROM PLAGUE TO FIRE

By the end of 1665, as the weather turned cold, people started to believe that the plague was finally ending. It would return in 1666 outside London, but over the winter London's streets once again became the noisy, bustling places they had been before the disease had arrived.

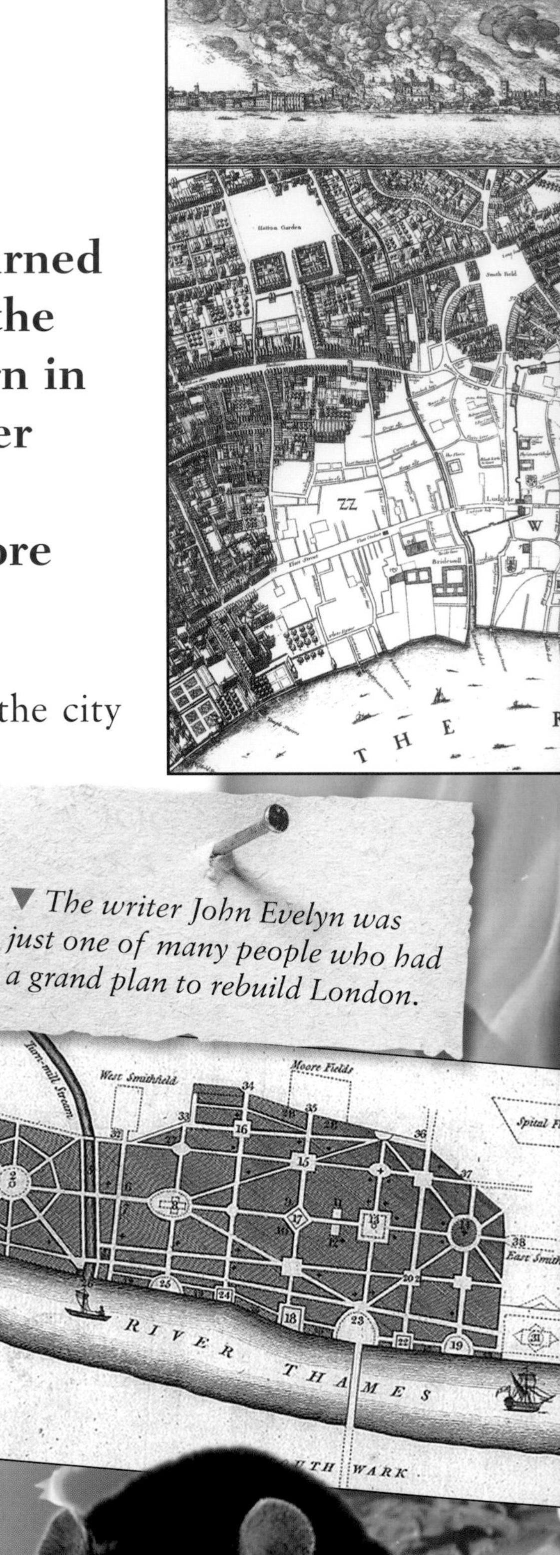

▼ *The writer John Evelyn was just one of many people who had a grand plan to rebuild London.*

The rich and lucky survivors who now returned to the city could not have seen the future. They could not have known that the Great Plague of 1665 would be the last major plague to strike London. No one can be sure why London was not struck down with any more plagues. Perhaps the answer lies in another disaster that hit the city?

London's burning

In the first week of September 1666, a fire started in a bakery on Pudding Lane. The fire destroyed everything in its path, including 13,200 houses. Londoners had rebuilt their lives after the plague; now they had to rebuild their city.

Starting over

Some people believe that the fire killed off the plague and ensured it would never return. The new streets of the city were certainly less cramped and dirty, but they cannot explain the end of plague on their own. After all, London was still home to the flea-infested rats that brought the plague in the first place.

This map was drawn just after the Great Fire. The white parts show how much of the city was destroyed by fire.

London's packed buildings helped the fierce fire to spread quickly, just as the plague had in 1665.

Tracking the Plague Around the World

When the plague left England in 1667, doctors and officials were no closer to understanding how the disease spread, or to finding a cure. They expected it to return.

Plague epidemics continued across Europe until 1720 when the disease struck another ancient port – Marseilles in southern France. The disease killed about 40,000 people, almost half the population of the city and surrounding areas.

A global killer

The bubonic plague, which was first recorded in the sixth century, left its terrible mark around the world for well over a thousand years. Several cities in India were struck in the 1800s. In 1850, a plague epidemic started in China that would spread from Hong Kong and other ports around the world. Cape Town, South Africa and San Francisco, USA, were hit in 1900.

The plague killed millions of people worldwide, but this time scientists believed they knew enough to stop it.

▶ *This plague doctor from Marseilles in 1720 is shown with smoke coming out of his nose case.*

Dr Bertrand tended the sick during the Marseilles plague of 1720. He wrote:

"Every house, every street, every alley resounds with sighs and groans. Terror lives in every heart and is stamped on every face."

◀ *This painting shows bodies being removed from the streets during the plague in Marseilles.*

▼ *These American volunteers are tackling a plague outbreak in China during 1914.*

CURING THE PLAGUE

Alexandre Yersin

During the 1800s, scientists had discovered that infectious diseases were not caused by bad air or by poison inside the victims' bodies. Diseases are caused by tiny germs or micro-organisms, too small to be seen without a microscope, that invade our bodies.

Microscopic mystery

As the plague epidemic swept out of China in the 1890s, the race was on to find the micro-organism that caused the plague. In 1894, French scientist Alexandre Yersin set off for plague-ridden Hong Kong, where he isolated the deadly germ.

The next step was to work out how humans caught the plague. Scientists proved that rat fleas, which jumped from rats to humans, carried the disease. Ships carried these rats and their fleas around the world.

Beating the plague

The riddle of the plague had been solved but there was still no cure. In the 1930s, the discovery of antibiotics that kill off disease-causing bacteria finally provided a possible cure for the disease that had cost countless millions of lives through the centuries.

◀ Powerful microscopes enabled scientists to discover what causes diseases.

LA
Le docteur Yersin v

▼ A French magazine shows Alexandre Yersin vaccinating patients against the plague.

Huit pages : Cl

Petit Parisien

SUPPLÉMENT LITTÉRAIRE ILLUSTRÉ

DIRECTION : 18, rue d'Enghien, PARIS

TOUS LES JEUDIS
SUPPLÉMENT LITTÉRAIRE
5 CENTIMES

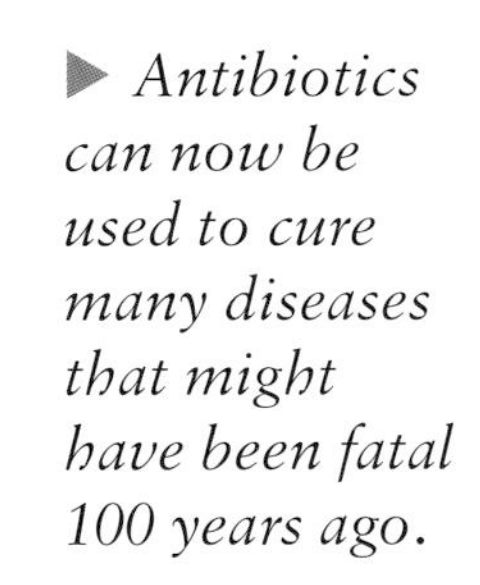

ISON DE LA PESTE ASIATIQUE
ant les Pestiférés de l'hôpital d'Amoy, en Chine

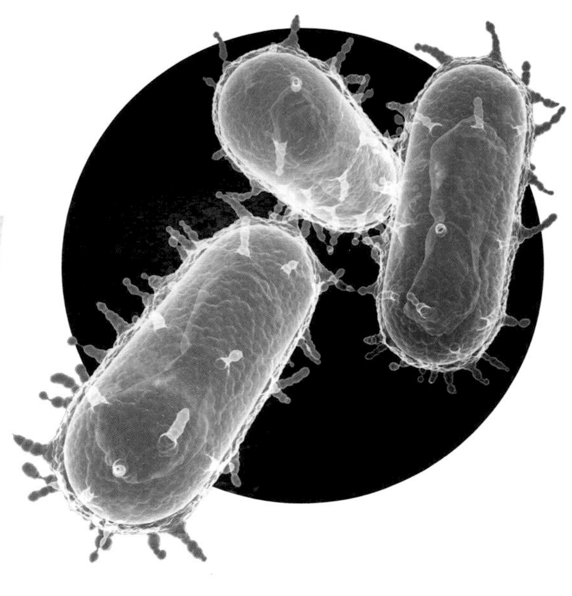

▲ This is what the micro-organism that causes the plague looks like under a microscope.

▶ Antibiotics can now be used to cure many diseases that might have been fatal 100 years ago.

Plague facts

In 1920, around 170,000 people around the world died of plague every year. By 1950, after the discovery of antibiotics, the disease claimed less than 5,000 lives.

LOOKING FOR CLUES

Even in the dirt and noise of the modern city, it is hard to imagine the filthy, rat-infested streets of London in 1665. What would it be like to see the beaked mask and the wax robe of the plague doctor, or to hear the ghostly sound of the plague bell in the smoke-filled alleyways?

Memorials and other objects that survive from the plague can help us to discover more about life and death during the Great Plague and other plague epidemics around the world.

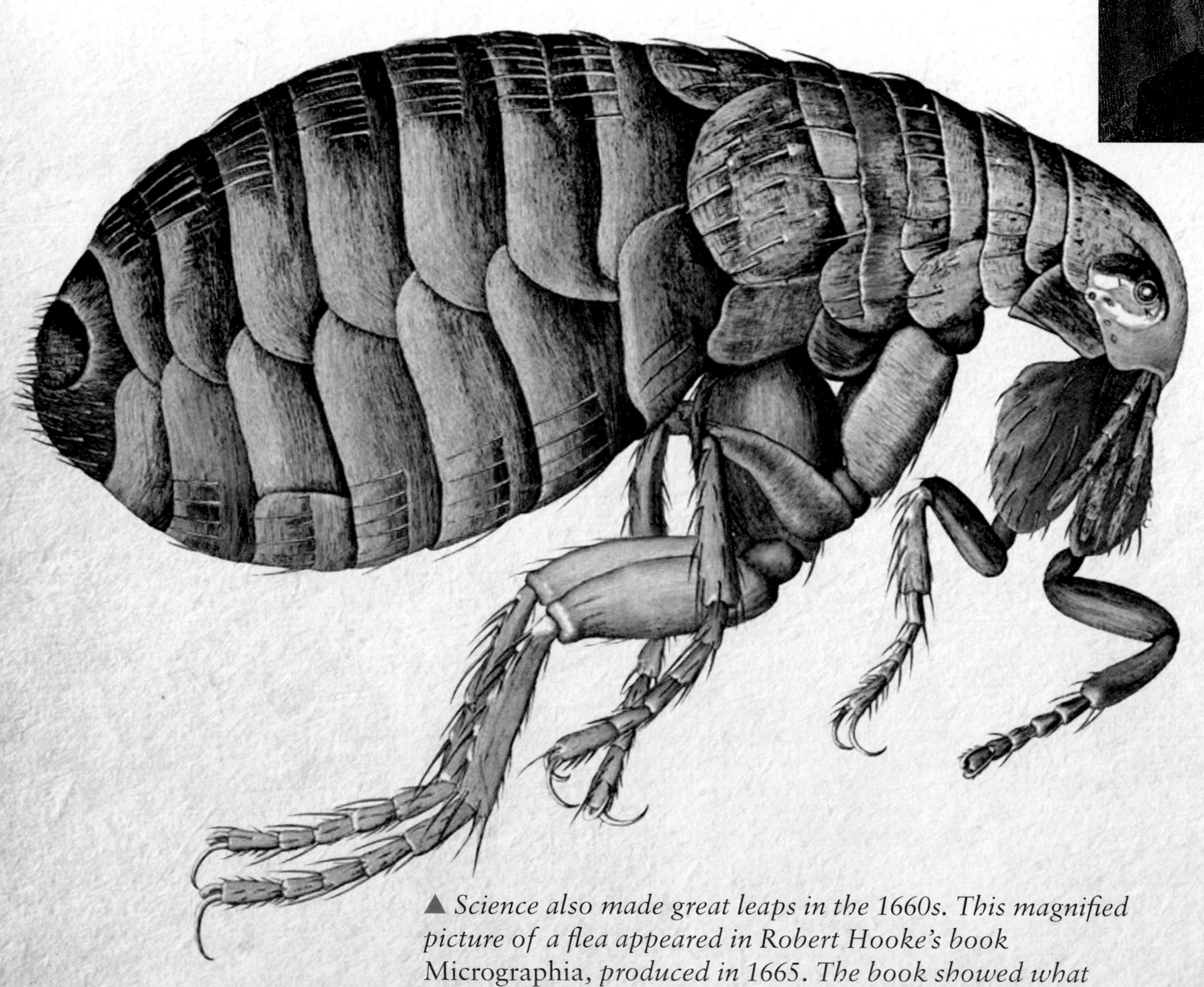

▲ *Science also made great leaps in the 1660s. This magnified picture of a flea appeared in Robert Hooke's book* Micrographia, *produced in 1665. The book showed what Hooke had discovered with one of the first microscopes. The discoveries of Hooke and others would lay the foundations for the prevention and cure of the plague.*

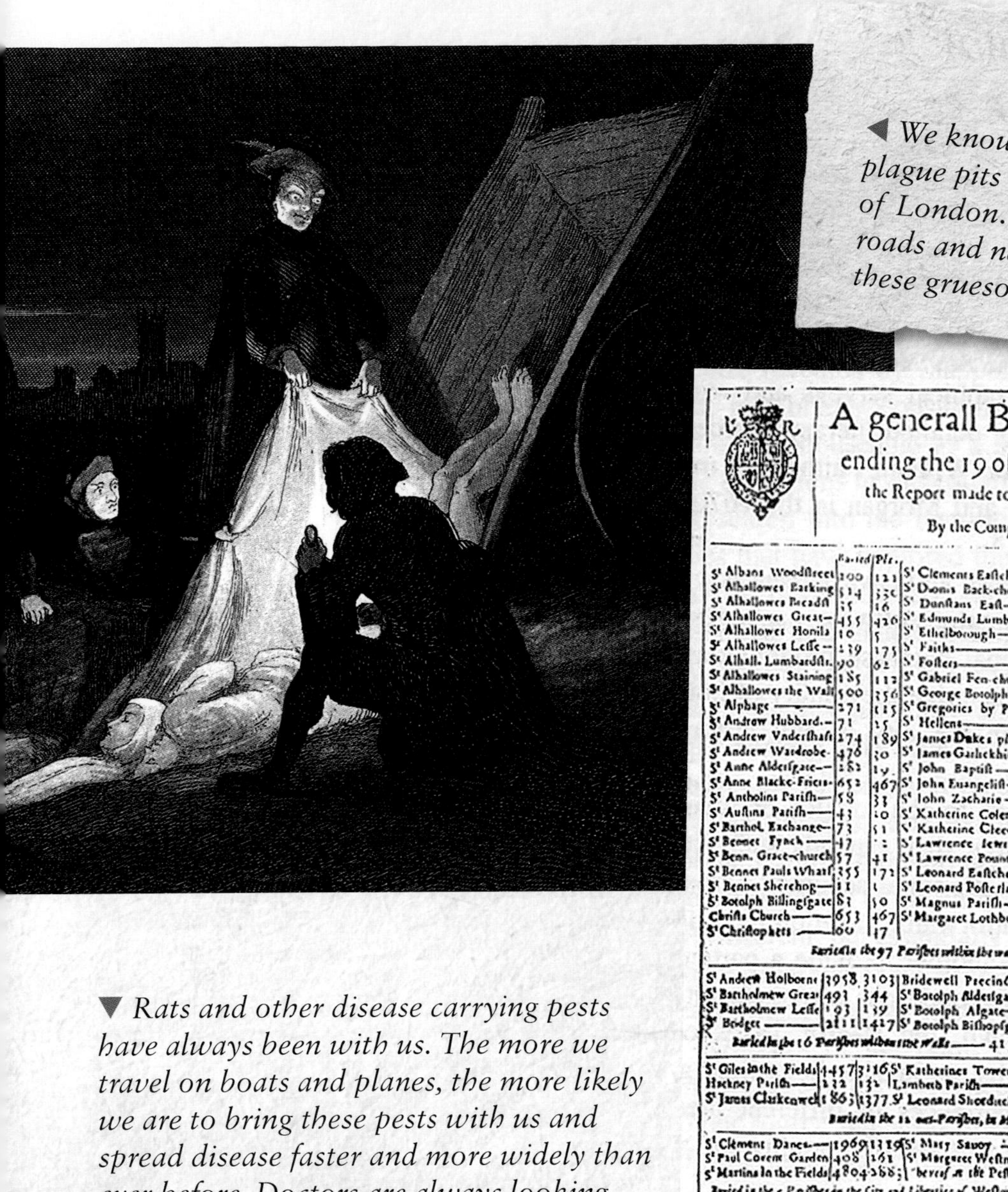

◀ *We know where many of the plague pits were dug around the edges of London. As the city has grown, roads and new buildings have covered these gruesome sites.*

A generall Bill for this present year, ending the 19 of *December* 1665. according to the Report made to the KINGS most Excellent Majesty.

By the Company of Parish Clerks of *London*, &c.

	Buried	Pla.		Buried	Pla.		Buried	Pla.		Buried	Pla.
St Albans Woodstreet	200	121	St Clements Eastcheap	38	20	St Margaret Moses	38	25	St Michael Cornhill	104	52
St Alhallowes Barking	514	330	St Dionis Back-church	78	27	St Margaret Newfishst	114	66	St Michael Crookedla.	179	133
St Alhallowes Breadst	35	16	St Dunstans East	265	150	St Margaret Pattons	49	24	St Michael Queenhit	203	122
St Alhallowes Great	455	426	St Edmunds Lumbard.	70	36	St Mary Abchurch	99	54	St Michael Que ne	44	18
St Alhallowes Honila	10	5	St Ethelborough	195	106	St Mary Aldermanbury	181	109	St Michael Royall	152	116
St Alhallowes Lesse	239	175	St Faiths	104	70	St Mary Aldermary	105	75	St Michael Woodstreet	122	62
St Alhall. Lumbardstr.	90	62	St Fosters	144	105	St Mary le Bow	64	36	St Mildred Breadstreet	59	26
St Alhallowes Staining	185	112	St Gabriel Fen-church	69	39	St Mary Bothaw	55	30	St Mildred Poultrey	68	46
St Alhallowes the Wall	500	356	St George Botolphlane	41	27	St Mary Colechurch	17	6	St Nicholas Acons	46	28
St Alphage	271	115	St Gregories by Pauls	376	232	St Mary Hill	94	64	St Nicholas Coleabby	125	91
St Andrew Hubbard	71	25	St Hellens	108	75	St Mary Mounthaw	56	37	St Nicholas Olaues	90	62
St Andrew Vndershaft	274	189	St James Dukes place	262	190	St Mary Summersset	342	262	St Olaves Hartstreet	237	160
St Andrew Wardrobe	476	30[illegible]	St James Garlickhithe	189	118	St Mary Staynings	47	27	St Olaves Iewry	54	32
St Anne Aldersgate	282	19[illegible]	St John Baptist	138	83	St Mary Woolchurch	65	33	St Olaves Silverstreete	250	132
St Anne Blacke-Friers	652	467	St John Euangelist	9		St Mary Woolnoth	75	38	St Pancras Soperlane	30	15
St Antholins Parish	58	33	St John Zacharie	85	54	St Martins Iremonger.	21	11	St Peters Cheape	61	35
St Austins Parish	43	20	St Katherine Coleman	299	213	St Martins Ludgate	196	128	St Peters Cornehill	136	76
St Barthol. Exchange	73	51	St Katherine Creechu.	335	231	St Martins Orgars	110	71	St Peters Pauls Wharfe	114	86
St Bennet Fynch	47	[illegible]	St Lawrence Iewry	94	48	St Martins Outwitch	60	34	St Peters Poore	79	47
St Benn. Grace-church	57	41	St Lawrence Pountney	214	140	St Martins Vintrey	417	349	St Stevens Colmanst.	560	391
St Bennet Pauls Wharf	355	172	St Leonard Eastcheap	42	27	St Matthew Fridayst.	24	6	St Stevens Walbrooke	34	17
St Bennet Sherehog	11	1	St Leonard Fosterlane	335	255	St Maudlins Milkstreet	44	22	St Swithins	93	56
St Botolph Billingsgate	83	50	St Magnus Parish	103	60	St Maudlins Oldfishst.	176	121	St Thomas Apostle	163	110
Christs Church	653	467	St Margaret Lothbury	100	66	St Michael Bassishaw	253	164	Trinitie Parish	115	79
St Christophers	60	47									

Buried in the 97 Parishes within the walls, — 15207 *Whereof, of the Plague* — 9887

St Andrew Holborne	3958	3103	Bridewell Precinct	230	179	St Dunstans West	958	665	St Saviours Southwark	4235	3446
St Bartholmew Great	493	344	St Botolph Aldersga.	997	755	St George Southwark	1613	1260	St Sepulchres Parish	4509	2746
St Bartholmew Lesse	193	139	St Botolph Algate	4926	4051	St Giles Cripplegate	8069	4838	St Thomas Southwark	475	371
St Bridget	2111	1427	St Botolph Bishopsg.	3464	2500	St Olaves Southwark	4793	2785	Trinity Minories	168	123
									At the Pesthouse	159	156

Buried in the 16 Parishes without the Walls — 41351 *Whereof, of the Plague* — 28888

St Giles in the Fields	4457	3216	St Katherines Tower	956	601	St Magdalen Bermon.	1943	1363	St Mary Whitechappel	4766	3855
Hackney Parish	232	132	Lambeth Parish	798	537	St Mary Newington	1272	1004	Redriffe Parish	304	210
St James Clarkenwel	1863	1377	St Leonard Shoreditch	2669	1949	St Mary Islington	696	593	Stepney Parish	8598	6583

Buried in the 12 out-Parishes, in Middlesex and Surrey — 28554 *Whereof, of the Plague* — 21420

St Clement Danes	1969	1319	St Mary Savoy	303	198
St Paul Covent Garden	408	261	St Margaret Westminst.	4710	3742
St Martins in the Fields	4804	2883	Whereof at the Pesthouse		156

Buried in the 5 Parishes in the City and Liberties of Westminster — 12194
Whereof, of the Plague — 8403

The Total of all the Christnings — 9967
The Total of all the Burials this year — 97306
Whereof, of the Plague — 68596

The Diseases and Casualties this year.

Abortive and Stilborne	617	Executed	21	Palsie	30
Aged	1545	Flox and Small Pox	655	Plague	68596
Ague and Feaver	5257	Found dead in streets, fields, &c.	20	Planner	6
Appoplex and Suddenly	116	French Pox	86	Plurisie	15
Bedrid	10	Frighted	23	Poysoned	1
Blasted	5	Gout and Sciatica	27	Quinsie	35
Bleeding	16	Grief	46	Rickets	557
Bloody Flux, Scowring & Flux	185	Griping in the Guts	1288	Rising of the Lights	397
Burnt and Scalded	8	Hangd & made away themselves	7	Rupture	34
Calenture	3	Headmouldshot & Mouldfallen	14	Scurvy	105
Cancer, Gangrene and Fistula	56	Jaundies	110	Shingles and Swine pox	2
Canker, and Thrush	111	Impostume	227	Sores, Ulcers, broken and bruised Limbs	82
Childbed	625	Kild by severall accidents	46	Spleen	14
Chrisomes and Infants	1258	Kings Evill	86	Spotted Feaver and Purples	1929
Cold and Cough	68	Leprosie	2	Stopping of the stomack	332
Collick and Winde	134	Lethargy	14	Stone and Strangury	98
Consumption and Tissick	4808	Livergrown	20	Surfet	1251
Convulsion and Mother	2036	Meagrom and Headach	12	Teeth and Worms	2614
Distracted	5	Measles	7	Vomiting	51
Dropsie and [illegible]	1478	Murthered and Shot	9	Wenn	[illegible]
[illegible]	50	Overlaid & Starved	45		

5114 / 4853 / 9967 — Males 48569 — Of the Plague 68596

in the 130 P[illegible]
in the 130 P[illegible]

▲ *This sheet shows the official numbers of plague victims in each part of London.*

▼ *Rats and other disease carrying pests have always been with us. The more we travel on boats and planes, the more likely we are to bring these pests with us and spread disease faster and more widely than ever before. Doctors are always looking for new cures so that scenes like the Great Plague of 1665, never happen again.*

Do people still catch the plague?

The plague is still with us. The disease kills around 200 people every year, mostly in poorer countries where people do not have access to the right medicines. Even in richer countries like the USA, about seven people still catch the plague every year.

▲ *Medical researchers are fighting a constant battle to stay one step ahead of changing micro-organisms that cause disease.*

Plague epidemics like the Black Death in the 1300s and the Great Plague of 1665 are a thing of the past. Like many diseases, the plague has been defeated by modern medicine. However, some scientists believe there is a risk that the plague could become resistant to modern antibiotics, and once again become a deadly killer.

▲ *Today, mosquitoes and not fleas are the world's biggest killer.*

Today's plagues

The plague may currently be under control, but the people who work to protect us from diseases can never relax. There are many diseases around the world that do just as much damage.

HIV/AIDS has killed 25 million people around the world since it was discovered 30 years ago. The search is still on for a cure but the disease can be prevented and drugs can help to slow down its effects. Many of the victims are in Africa, where they do not have access to the knowledge or the drugs to fight this modern plague.

Plague facts

Some countries have created biological weapons to spread diseases in enemy cities. Plague bacteria have been included in these weapons and may even have been used during World War II.

▲ *Chemicals are sprayed to combat mosquitoes that carry modern plagues such as malaria and dengue fever.*

▲ *Members of the US Navy test breathing equipment that could be used during a biological attack.*

▲ *The streets of London have changed since 1665. Governments still have to be alert to the risks of old and new diseases in crowded cities.*

PLAGUE TIMELINE

AD 542 The plague of Justinian spreads from Egypt to Constantinople, one of the first recorded plague outbreaks.

1345 Plague-ridden bodies are thrown into the city of Kaffa, on the shores of the Black Sea, in an early form of biological warfare.

1348 The Black Death arrives in Western Europe, killing around one-third of the population.

1563 A plague outbreak kills nearly a quarter of London's population.

1651 Astrologer William Lilly produces an engraving that seems to predict London's plague and fire.

1663 Plague breaks out in Holland, causing 35,000 deaths in the capital city Amsterdam.

1665

May: 43 deaths from plague in poor areas of London.

7 June: Samuel Pepys notices houses in Drury Lane marked with red crosses to show they are infected with plague.

20 June: Weekly plague deaths pass 100 for the first time.

5 July: Pepys sends his wife to stay outside London.

9 July: King Charles II and his royal court move to Hampton Court Palace, to the west of London.

24 July: Weekly plague deaths pass 1,000.

6 September: Tailor George Vicars becomes the first person to die of plague in the Derbyshire village of Eyam.

26 September: Plague deaths in London reach their peak, with 7,165 victims over the previous week.

December: Many Londoners who had left the city finally return as the cold weather ends the plague epidemic.

1666

June: Plague deaths increase in Eyam and clergyman William Mompesson persuades the villagers to shut themselves off from the outside world.

2 September: The Great Fire of London breaks out, destroying the last traces of plague in the city.

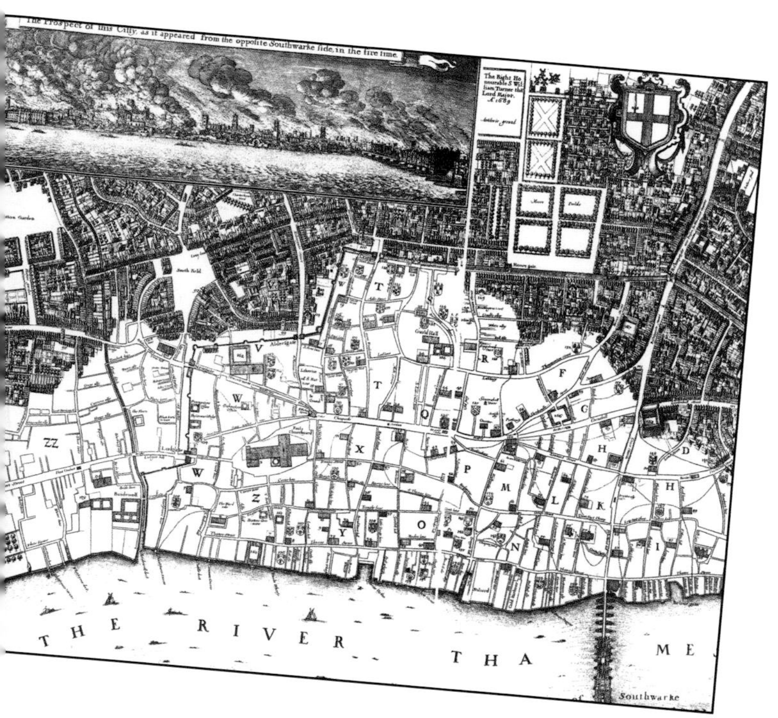

1720

The Great Plague of Marseilles, France kills around half of the city's population.

1722 Daniel Defoe publishes a fictional account of the Great Plague of London, *A Journal of the Plague Year*.

1850 The last Great Plague epidemic starts to claim lives in China, later spreading from China around the world.

1894 The plague-causing micro-organism is isolated by Alexandre Yersin during a plague outbreak in Hong Kong.

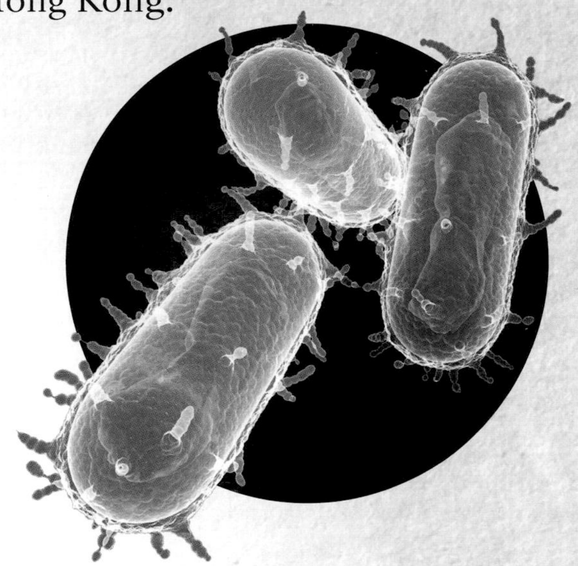

1897 Japanese scientist Masanori Ogata shows that plague is carried and spread by rat fleas.

1900 Plague epidemics strike in San Francisco, USA and Cape Town, South Africa.

1930s The discovery of antibiotics finally provides an effective cure for the plague, if taken within the first few days of infection.

Glossary

behead kill someone by cutting off their head

Bill of Mortality weekly publication in seventeenth century London that gave details of the numbers of people dying and their causes of death

biological weapon weapon that uses germs to attack people

Black Death the outbreak of plague that swept across Europe in the 1300s, killing as many as one in three people

boil swelling on the skin filled with pus

charnel house a building where human remains are stored

clergyman people who are able to provide services to members of a Christian church. In the 1660s, these people were always men

comet lump of ice and rock that shines brightly in the sky when it comes near the Sun

English Civil War conflict between supporters of King Charles I and forces of parliament that resulted in Charles I being executed in 1649

epidemic disease that infects lots of people in a short time

fever when a person's body temperature is higher than normal

germ micro-organism that can cause disease such as bacteria or viruses

gland small organs in the body which often become swollen when a person is ill

HIV/AIDS disease caused by a virus that affects victims' immune systems so they are more likely to catch other diseases

leech type of worm that sucks blood from bodies it bites. Leeches were often used in the past by doctors to take blood from patients

lozenge a small medicated tablet which dissolves in the mouth

micro-organism tiny living thing such as bacteria or viruses that can only be seen through a microscope

microscope powerful magnifying tool that enables us to view things that are too small to see with the naked eye

mystic someone who claims or appears to have magical powers, such as predicting the future

omen sign of what is to happen in the future

pamphlet small book without a hard cover or binding

pest house type of hospital where plague victims were sent. Medical care in pest houses was often very primitive and many who were sent there were simply left to die

plague pit mass grave where many bodies were buried during times of plague

pneumonic plague infectious disease that can be passed from one body to another through the air

potion mixture made up to cure disease, often with no medical value

quack someone claiming to be a doctor with little or no medical training

quarantine keep someone or something isolated, in order to check if it is infected with disease. The aim is to stop the accidental spread of disease

trade buying and selling goods, particularly to and from different countries with goods being carried by ship

vaccinate injecting people with a tiny dose of a disease, so their bodies can learn to fight off the illness and become protected from catching the disease

vomiting being sick

FIND OUT MORE

Books

The Great Plague – A London Girl's Diary (My Story series)
by Pamela Oldfield (Scholastic, 2008)
A fictional diary telling one girl's story of life during the plague.

Plagues, Pox and Pestilence
by Richard Platt and John Kelly (Kingfisher, 2011)
A history of plague and other diseases.

The Story of London
by Jacqui Bailey and Christopher Maynard (A & C Black, 2000)

Plague and Peril (Horrible Histories series)
by Terry Deary and Martin Brown (Scholastic, 2009)

Plague: A Cross on the Door
by Ann Turnbull (A & C Black, 2013)

Online resources

The National Archives website includes a lesson and sources about the Great Plague.
www.nationalarchives.gov.uk/education/lesson49.htm

The Museum of London is a great place to visit if you want to find out more about the city's past. This website gives a history of plagues in London.
www.museumoflondon.org.uk/Explore-online/Pocket-histories/plagues

The British Library website includes source material about the plague.
www.bl.uk/learning/histcitizen/uk/plague/plague1665.html

Samuel Pepys is an important figure from the time of the Great Plague. This BBC website tells his life story for younger readers.

www.bbc.co.uk/schools/famouspeople/standard/pepys/index

The Science Museum's website on the history of medicine includes a section about the Black Death.

www.sciencemuseum.org.uk/broughttolife/themes/diseases/black_death

Read more about the amazing story of Eyam.

www.eyamplaguevillage.co.uk

You could also visit a local museum to find out if your town was hit by the plague in 1665–1666 or during the Black Death of the 1340s.

A The National Archives

The National Archives is the UK government's official archive containing over 1,000 years of history. They give detailed guidance to government departments and the public sector on information management, and advise others about the care of historical archives.

www.nationalarchives.gov.uk

National Archives picture acknowledgements and catalogue references

p5, p25 and p33 PROB 1/9. Samuel Pepys signature.

p15 SP 29/122 f.185. Proposal for the prevention of the plague.

p18-19 SP 29/155 f.142. Decree of plague rules and regulations.

p20 SP 16.484.15s1. An earlier decree of plague rules from 1641.

p23 SP 29/126/f.65. Page from a prayer book written specially for times of plague.

p23 SP29.132.28. Letter by journalist Henry Muddiman.

p29 SP 29/134 f.31. Letter from Thomas Povey written 8 October 1665.

p48 ZMAP4_18. Map of area of London destroyed by great fire.

Index

Picture acknowledgements

Front cover images: Background ZMAP4_18 ©The National Archives, all montage images ©Shutterstock aside from PROB4/5288 ©The National Archives and ©Bettmann/Corbis.
Back cover images: Background ZMAP4_18 ©The National Archives, all montage images Wikimedia or Shutterstock.
Inside images all Shutterstock, aside from the following: p1 background ZMAP4_18 ©The National Archives, p4 ©Bettmann/Corbis, p5 top right John Hayls (1600–1679) Wikimedia, p5 signature inset PROB1/9 ©The National Archives, p5 bottom ©Heritage Images/Corbis, p6 bottom centre Wikimedia, p7 top inset ©Corbis, p8 inset centre ©Anna Hoychuk/Shutterstock, p9 ©Bettmann/Corbis, p10-11 Wikimedia, p11 inset ©Lebrecht 3/Lebrecht Music & Arts/Corbis, p12 top inset ©Michael Nicholson/Corbis, p12 bottom inset ©Georgios Kollidas/Shutterstock, p13 ©Heritage Images/Corbis, p14 ©Mary Evans Picture Library, p15 top Wenceslaus Hollar/Wikimedia, p15 bottom SP 29/122 f.185 ©The National Archives, p16 inset John Hayls (1600–1679) Wikimedia, p16-17 ©Bettmann/Corbis, p17 top right inset ©Bettmann/Corbis, p17 top centre inset Wikimedia, p18 inset ©Nicole Duplaix/Corbis, p18-19 SP 29/155 f.142 ©The National Archives, p19 top inset ©Wellcome Images, p20 inset SP 16.484.15s1 ©The National Archives, p20-21 ©Heritage Images/Corbis, p21 Wikimedia, p22 bottom left ©Maljalen/Shutterstock, p23 SP 29/126/f.65 and SP 29.132.28 The National Archives, p24 bottom left ©Museum of London, p24 centre Frederic Shields (1870) Wikimedia, p24-25 background ©LianeM/Shutterstock p25 ©Michael Nicholson/Corbis, p25 signature inset PROB1/9 ©The National Archives, p26 ©haak78/Shutterstock, p27 bottom Wenceslaus Hollar/Wikimedia, p27 top ©Hulton Archive/Getty Images, p28 top ©Hulton Archive/Getty Images, p29 ©Universal History Archive/Getty Images, p29 background SP 29/134 f.31 ©The National Archives, p30 bottom inset ©SSPL/Getty Images, p30 top and p31 bottom ©Heritage Images/Corbis, p31 top right Hendrick Van der Borcht (d.1660) via Wikimedia, p32 top inset ©Universal History Archive/Getty Images, p32 bottom left ©Hulton Archive/Getty Images, p33 ©Historical Picture Archive/Getty Images, p35 Wikimedia, p35 top right ©Bettmann/Corbis, p37 Wikimedia, p38 ©Georgios Kollidas/Shutterstock, p39 ©SSPL/Getty Images, p39 top right inset ©Hulton Archive/Getty Images, p41 ©SSPL/Getty Images, p42 ©Dea/G. Cigolini/Veneranda Biblioteca Ambrosiana/De Agostini/Getty Images, p43 Wenceslaus Hollar/Wikimedia, p44 inset ©Museums Sheffield, p44-45 bottom ©Outnaboutonfoot via Flickr Creative Commons, p44-45 top Wikimedia, p45 left Wikimedia, p46 top inset ©Nicole Duplaix/Corbis, p47 bottom ©Danita Delimont/Getty Images, p47 top right ©Ralphrepo via Flickr Creative Commons, p48 inset John Evelyn/Wikimedia, p48-49 ZMAP4_18 ©The National Archives, p49 Universal History Archive/Getty Images, p50 bottom Wikimedia, p50-51 Wikimedia, p51 ©American Red Cross/National Geographic Society/Corbis, p52 top inset Wikimedia, p52-53 ©Lee/Leemage/Getty Images, p53 top inset ©Michael Taylor/Shutterstock, p54 Wikimedia, p55 top ©Universal History Archive/Getty Images, p55 right Wikimedia, p56 inset ©michaeljung/Shutterstock, p56-57 ©Campbell-Ewald via Flickr Creative Commons, p57 top ©mrfiza/Shutterstock, p57 bottom ©Bikeworldtravel/Shutterstock, p58 Wikimedia, p59 ZMAP4_18 ©The National Archives, p59 top left ©Michael Taylor/Shutterstock.